MORALITY AND BEYOND

D0896415

hARPER ✝ ᴄoRChBOOKS

*A reference-list of Harper Torchbooks, classified
by subjects, is printed at the end of this volume.*

Mary Ann Creadon

Publisher's Note

This Torchbook paperback edition reprints Volume IX of the RELIGIOUS PERSPECTIVES SERIES, *which is planned and edited by* RUTH NANDA ANSHEN. *Dr. Anshen's Epilogue to this reprint appears on page 97 ff.*

MORALITY
AND
BEYOND

by

Paul Tillich

HARPER TORCHBOOKS ❧ The Cloister Library
Harper & Row, Publishers, New York

to

REINHOLD NIEBUHR

MORALITY AND BEYOND

Copyright © 1963 by Paul Tillich.

Printed in the United States of America.

This book was originally published in 1963 by Harper & Row, Publishers,in the Religious Perspective Series edited by Ruth Nanda Anshen.

First HARPER TORCHBOOK edition published 1966 by
Harper & Row, Publishers, Incorporated
New York, N.Y. 10016.

Grateful acknowledgment is made to The University of Chicago Press to reprint Chapters IV and V of this book from *The Protestant Era* by Paul Tillich, published in 1948 and copyright 1948 by The University of Chicago. Chapter IV, "The Transmoral Conscience," originally appeared in *Crozer Quarterly*, Vol. XXII (1945), No. 4; Chapter V, "Ethics in a Changing World," originally appeared in *Religion and the Modern World* (Philadelphia: University of Pennsylvania Press, 1941).

Library of Congress Catalog Card Number: 63-18280.

CONTENTS

Introduction   13

1. The Religious Dimension of the Moral Imperative   17

2. The Religious Source of the Moral Demands   31

3. The Religious Element in Moral Motivation   47

4. The Transmoral Conscience   65

5. Ethics in a Changing World   82

Epilogue: Religious Perspectives:
Its Meaning and Purpose by Ruth Nanda Anshen   97

Introduction

Theological ethics is an element of systematic theology, present in each of its parts. As a matter of expediency, it is often treated separately in lectures and studies because of the immensity of the material to be covered and the justified desire, on the scholar's part, to deal with particular problems comprehensively. The problem to be discussed in the following five chapters is the age-old question of how the moral is related to the religious.

It is urgent to raise this question again in view of the present character both of the church's preaching and of philosophical ethics. The latter either shares the general retreat of analytical philosophy into logical and semantic problems or continues the discussion of value theory (which in itself is a retreat from ontological inquiry), or else it undermines the possibility of ethical norms by pure pragmatism or pure existentialism, although this assumption of purity is a delusion.

More important, however, is the state of preaching and teaching in the church, both Catholic and Protestant, and most conspicuously in Protestantism. The gospel (*euangelion,* "good news"), the message of reconciliation and reunion with God as the Ground and Aim of our being has been transformed into a multiplicity of laws, partly doctrinal and partly ethical. The moral "yoke" that Jesus wished to make easy has only been made heavier, and the message of grace has largely been lost, despite the numerous liturgical prayers for the forgiveness of sins. They do not express the vision that appears in

Paul's Letters and John's Gospel, or is expressed in the seventh petition of the Lord's Prayer—"save us from the evil one"—namely, the image of a demonic power ruling the universe and driving man into separation from God and into hostility against Him. The prayers for forgiveness have, for many people, only the function of relieving the uneasy conscience produced by trespasses against traditional and often absurd rules of behavior, mostly of a prohibitive character. But they do not express the great paradox, that there is a reunion with the eternal "Ground of our being" without "right" action on our part, without our being "good people," or the "people of good will." Therefore, despite liturgical formulae, hymns, and the reading of lessons from the Pauline Epistles, the message of grace has been lost. Grace as the power of accepting the person who is unacceptable, and of healing the person who is mortally sick, has disappeared behind the preaching of the religious and moral law.

It is understandable that people, in view of this graceless moralism, turn to secular ethics. But when they find nothing more than the logical analysis of ethical theory, they turn easily to a cynical relativism or to a totalitarian absolutism in ethics, each often a consequence of the other. The question implicit in this situation is: Can we point to something that transcends both graceless moralism and normless relativism in ethical theory and moral action?

The response of Christianity is the message that a new reality has appeared with the coming of the Christ, a power of being in which we can participate, and out of which true thought and right action can follow, however fragmentarily. We find analogous affirmations in other religions and even in secular movements of an implicitly religious character, such as nationalism, socialism, and liberal humanism. Being precedes action in everything that is, including man, although in man as the bearer of freedom, previous action also determines present being. This answer stands in opposition to both moral legalism and amoral lawlessness. It affirms morality and points beyond it to its religious foundation.

"Religious principles of moral action" is the subject matter of the first three chapters of this volume, which form a kind of unity, and were originally delivered under the same title as the Jacob Ziskind Memorial Lectures at Dartmouth College. The last two chapters, taken from my book *The Protestant Era*, discuss decisive consequences of the basic analysis—Chapter IV demonstrating the liberation of the moral conscience by its transmoral foundation, and Chapter V the possibility of conquering ethical relativism through the united principles of *agape* ("love") and *kairos* ("the right moment"). I am grateful to the University of Chicago Press for granting me permission to reprint these two chapters.

The manner in which this book has come into existence accounts for some repetition and for occasional incompleteness. Despite these limitations, it is my hope that the study will help to remove the obsolete conflict between reason-determined ethics and faith-determined ethics. It attempts to do so by showing that the religious principles dwell within the principles of moral action. If morality is intrinsically religious, as religion is intrinsically ethical, neither is dependent on the other, and neither can be substituted for the other.

I am deeply grateful to Mrs. Elizabeth Wood who has again improved my English style as she did for the three volumes of my sermons.

This book is dedicated to Reinhold Niebuhr, after thirty years of friendship and dialogue. The tension between the ethical, which he has represented, and the ontological, for which I have stood, has proved to be an important door by which to enter into the mysteries of theology and life.

Not forgotten is the decisive role he played in bringing my family and myself to the United States shortly after the Nazis came to power and forced me to leave Germany in 1933. Ever since, we have worked together in mutual support, criticism, and *agape*.

PAUL TILLICH

East Hampton, Long Island
July 1963

I

The Religious Dimension
of the Moral Imperative

In the first three chapters of this book, the immanence of the religious in the moral shall be considered from three directions. The first chapter deals with the religious *dimension* of the moral imperative, the second with the religious *source* of the moral demands, and the third with the religious *element* in moral motivation.

To understand the meaning of the phrase "moral imperative," we must distinguish the three basic functions of the human spirit: morality, culture, and religion. When we call them functions of man's "spirit," we point to the dynamic unity of body and mind, of vitality and rationality, of the conscious and the unconscious, of the emotional and the intellectual. In every function of the human spirit the whole person is involved, and not merely one part or one element. As I have often insisted, we must revive the term "spirit" as designating a natural quality of man. It cannot be replaced by "mind" because "mind" is overweighted by its intellectual aspect.

None of the three functions of the spirit ever appears in isolation from the other two. They must be distinguished, nonetheless, because they are able to relate to each other in many different ways. Most concisely, we might say: morality is the constitution of the bearer of the spirit, the centered person;

culture points to the creativity of the spirit and also to the totality of its creations; and religion is the self-transcendence of the spirit toward what is ultimate and unconditioned in being and meaning.

The first of these functions is our direct and primary subject. But in order to deal with it adequately we must continually refer to the other two. This presents a difficulty hardly to be resolved in an essay such as this, and only overcome within a system that comprises the whole of man's interpretation of himself and the meaning of his life (which I undertook to develop in my *Systematic Theology*). The present study must presuppose but cannot develop such an interpretation; however, we must refer to it, and derive from it a possible solution of the problem at hand—"the religious principles of moral action."

The moral act establishes man as a person, and as a bearer of the spirit. It is the unconditional character of the moral imperative that gives ultimate seriousness both to culture and to religion. Without it culture would deteriorate into an aesthetic or utilitarian enterprise, and religion into an emotional distortion of mysticism. It was the prophetic message, as recorded in the Old Testament, that contrasted the moral imperative, in terms of the demand for justice, with both the culture and the religion of its time. The message is one of ultimate seriousness and has no equivalent in any other religion. The seriousness of Christianity depends upon it, as does also any ultimate seriousness in Western culture. Science and the arts, politics, education—all become empty and self-destructive if, in their creation, the moral imperative is disregarded. The imperative exhibits itself in scientific and artistic honesty to the extent of self-sacrifice; in one's commitment to humanity and justice in social relations and political actions; and in the love of one toward the other, as a consequence of experiencing the divine love. These are examples which demonstrate that, without the immanence of the moral imperative, both culture and religion disintegrate because of lack of ultimate seriousness.

The moral imperative is the command to become what one potentially is, a *person* within a community of persons. Only man, in the limit of our experience, can become a person, because only man is a completely centered self, having himself as a self in the face of a world to which he belongs and from which he is, at the same time, separated. This dual relation to his world, belongingness and separation, makes it possible for him to ask questions and find answers, to receive and make demands. As a centered self and individual, man can respond in knowledge and action to the stimuli that reach him from the world to which he belongs; but because he also *confronts* his world, and in this sense is free from it, he can respond "responsibly," namely, after deliberation and decision rather than through a determined compulsion. This is his greatness, but also his danger: it enables him to act *against* the moral demand. He can surrender to the disintegrating forces which tend to control the personal center and to destroy its unity. But before we pursue this line of thought, we must consider more thoroughly some of our concepts up to this point.

Man has a world, namely, a structured whole of innumerable parts, a *cosmos,* as the Greeks called it, because of its structured character which makes it accessible to man through acts of creative receiving and transforming. Having a world is more than having environment. Of course, man, like any other being, has environment; but in contrast to the higher animals, for example, he is not bound to it. He can transcend it in any direction, in imagination, thought and action (e.g., social utopias or ontological concepts or space exploration). Man has "world" through every part of his environment. His encounter with any of the objects surrounding him is always an encounter with the universe manifest in a particular object. Man never encounters *this* tree only as *this* tree, but also as *tree,* one of many trees, as an example of the species tree (in itself a special manifestation of the universal power of being).

Such an encounter presupposes freedom from the particular, and the ability to see the universal within the particular. The manifestation of this freedom is language. Language lives in universals. It is one and the same thing to have world, to transcend environment, and to speak in concepts and meaningful propositions. All this constitutes man's essential freedom and is the presupposition of man's experience of the moral imperative.

The moral imperative is the demand to become actually what one is essentially and therefore potentially. It is the power of man's being, given to him by nature, which he shall actualize in time and space. His true being shall become his actual being—this is the moral imperative. And since his true being is the being of a person in a community of persons, the moral imperative has this content: to become a person. Every moral act is an act in which an individual self establishes itself as a person.

Therefore, a moral act is not an act in obedience to an external law, human or divine. It is the inner law of our true being, of our essential or created nature, which demands that we actualize what follows from it. And an antimoral act is not the transgression of one or several precisely circumscribed commands, but an act that contradicts the self-realization of the person as a person and drives toward disintegration. It disrupts the centeredness of the person by giving predominance to partial trends, passions, desires, fears, and anxieties. The central control is weakened, often almost removed. And when this happens, and other partial trends also aspire to predominance, the self is split, and the conflicting trends make it their battlefield. The "will," in the sense of a self that acts from the centered totality of its being, is enslaved. Freedom is replaced by compulsion. Deliberation and decision, the hallmarks of freedom, become mere façades for overwhelming drives that predetermine the decision. The voice of man's essential being is silenced, step by step; and his disintegrating self, his depersonalization, shows the nature of the antimoral act and, by contrast, the nature of the moral act.

The moral act as the self-actualization of the centered self or the constitution of the person as a person, has analogies in the realm of all living beings, including man from the biological point of view. The analogy to the diminution or loss of centeredness in man is the psychosomatic phenomenon of disease. In disease, some processes that are necessary elements in the whole of a life process take an independent course and endanger the functioning of the whole. The cancerous growth of parts of the body is the most illuminating analogy to what happens in the centered self when particular trends conquer the center and destroy the unity of balanced trends. The analogy between the antimoral act and bodily disease is in many (somehow in all) cases more than an analogy. Both are expressions of the universal ambiguity of life, according to which the processes of self-integration are continuously combated by movements toward disintegration. For the ethical problem this means that the moral act is always a victory over disintegrating forces and that its aim is the actualization of man as a centered and therefore free person.

At this point a short semantic remark seems necessary. In this study, I use the terms "morality," "morals," and "moral" throughout most of the text. And sometimes the term "ethical" appears. There would be no confusion if, as I now suggest, we defined ethics as the "science of the moral." But this is not a generally accepted definition, the chief reason being that the word "moral," through historical accidents, has received several distorting connotations. Since the eighteenth century, at least in Europe, it has carried the implication of "moralism" in the sense of graceless legalistic ethics. And in the United States, it has, under the influence of Puritanism, taken on a sexual signification: to be "amoral" means to be sexually lawless, or at least to deny conventional sex ethics. Because of these two connotations, one has tried to replace "moral" by "ethical." Were this generally accepted, however, the term "ethical" would soon acquire the connotation of "moral," and there would be no change. Therefore, I recommend that "ethical" be reserved for the *theory* of morals, and that the term "moral" and its derivatives be purged of those associations, and used to describe the moral act itself in its fundamental significance.

We have discussed the nature of the moral act, its all-permeating character, and its immanence in the other two chief functions of man's spirit—the cultural and the religious. We must now ask: what is the religious dimension of the moral imperative, and (in Chapter II) what is the relation of cultural creativity to morality?

In answer to the first question, we can say: the religious dimension of the moral imperative is its unconditional character. This, of course, leads to a subsequent question: why is the moral imperative unconditional, and in which respects can one call it so, and in which not? In our daily life we use innumerable imperatives; but most of them are conditional: "you ought to leave *now,* if you wish to catch your plane." But perhaps you prefer to stay, even though you miss the plane. This obviously is a conditional imperative. However, if getting to the plane should be a matter of life and death, as, for example, in the case of a physician who must immediately operate upon a patient, the conditional imperative becomes unconditional. To miss the plane through negligence would then be an antimoral act, and would affect the person of the physician in a disintegrating manner. We might compare the disintegrating effect that the failure to save a drowning woman has on the main character in Camus' *The Fall*.

There are many cases in which conditional imperatives have some bearing on an unconditional imperative. The missing of the plane might also arouse anxiety in those who expect the arrival of a friend. And there are cases in which several imperatives compete for supreme validity, and in which the decision is a moral risk. But despite these "mixed" cases, the moral imperative in itself is, as Immanuel Kant called it, "categorical" rather than "hypothetical," or as I would say, unconditional as opposed to conditional.

We may ask, however, whether a moral decision can stand under an unconditional imperative if the decision is a moral risk—the "risk" implying that it might prove to be the wrong decision. The answer to this question is that the unconditional character does not refer to the content, but to the form of the moral decision. Whichever side of a moral alternative might be chosen, however great the risk in a bold decision may be, if it be a *moral* decision it is dependent only on the pure "ought to be" of the moral imperative. And should anyone be in doubt as to which of several possible acts conforms to the moral imperative, he should be reminded that each of them might be justified in a particular situation, but that whatever he chooses must be done with the consciousness of standing under an unconditional imperative. The doubt concerning the justice of a moral act does not contradict the certainty of its ultimate seriousness.

The assertion of the intrinsically religious character of the moral imperative can be criticized from different points of view. Theology can strongly affirm the unconditioned character of the moral imperative, but deny that this character makes it religious. Moral commands, one argues then, are religious because they are divine commandments. They are ultimately serious because they express the "Will of God."

This alone makes them unconditional. God could have willed differently, and we must open our eyes to His revelation in order to know what His Will actually is. Such an argument, of course, would exclude any kind of secular ethics. Not only the content but also the unconditional character of the moral imperative would have to be sanctioned by a divine command, and conserved in holy traditions or sacred books.

I maintain, however, that the term "Will of God" can and must be understood differently. It is not an external will imposed upon us, an arbitrary law laid down by a heavenly tyrant, who is strange to our essential nature and therefore whom we resist justifiably from the point of view of our nature. The "Will of God" for us is precisely our essential being with all its potentialities, our created nature declared as "very good" by God, as, in terms of the Creation myth, He "saw everything that he made." For us the "Will of God" is manifest in our essential being; and only because of this can we accept the moral imperative as valid. It is not a strange law that demands our obedience, but the "silent voice" of our own nature as man, and as man with an individual character.

But we must go one further step. We can say: to fulfill one's own nature is certainly a moral demand intrinsic in one's being. But why is it an unconditional imperative? Do I not have the right to leave my potentialities unfulfilled, to remain less than a person, to contradict my essential goodness, and thus to destroy myself? As a being that has the freedom of self-contradiction, I should have the right to this possibility, and to waste myself! The moral imperative is unconditional only if I choose to affirm my own essential nature, and *this is* a condition! The answer to this argument is the experience that has been expressed in the doctrine of the infinite value of every human soul in the view of the Eternal. It is not an external prohibition against self-destruction— bodily, psychologically, or morally—that we experience in states of despair, but the silent voice of our own being which denies us the right to self-destruction. It is the awareness of our belonging to a dimension that transcends our own finite freedom and our ability to affirm or to negate ourselves. So I maintain my basic assertion that the unconditional character of the moral imperative is its religious quality. No religious heteronomy, subjection to external commands, is implied if we maintain the immanence of religion in the moral command.

The intrinsically religious character of the moral imperative is indirectly denied by the philosophy of values. Its representatives think in terms of a hierarchy of values, in which the value of the holy may or may not find a place; when it does, it is often on the top of this pyramid, above the moral, legal, social, political, and economic values. For our problem, this means first of all that values lie above and below each other and that there can be no immanence of one within another. The value of the holy, for example. cannot be immanent in the value of the good, and conversely. The relationship is external and may lead to the elimination of one or the other —most frequently, in this case, the value of the holy.

A second character of the value theory has a considerable bearing on our problem. The establishment of values and their relationships presupposes a valuating subject, and the question arises: how can values that are relative to a valuating individual or group (e.g., pleasure values) be separated from values that are valid by their very nature regardless of personal or social attitudes? If there are such "absolute values" (absolute in the sense of being independent of a valuating subject), what is the source of their absoluteness, how can they be discovered, how are they related to reality, and what is their ontological standing? These questions lead unavoidably to a situation that the value theory by its very nature tries to avoid—namely, a doctrine of being, an ontology. For values have reality only if they are rooted in reality. Their validity is an expression of their ontological foundation. *Being precedes value,* but value fulfills being. Therefore, the value theory, in its search for absolute values, is thrown back upon the ontological question of the source of values in being.

A third way in which the religious dimension of the moral imperative is questioned can be described as the attempt, with the help of psychological and sociological explanations, to deny the unconditional character of the moral altogether. The psychological impact of realities like the demanding and threatening parents, or of doctrines like that of the commanding and punishing God, evokes the feeling of something unconditionally serious from which there is no escape and with which there can be no compromise.

The same argument can be strengthened by sociological considerations. For example, one can derive, like Nietzsche, the shaping of the conscience of the masses from centuries of pressure exercised by the ruling groups, who did not hesitate to employ all, even the most cruel, tools of suppression—military, legal, educational, psychological. From generation to generation this pressure produced an increasing internalization of commands, namely, the sense of standing under an inner unconditional command, an absolute moral imperative.

This type of argument seems convincing. But it is circular because it presupposes what it tries to prove—the identity of two qualitatively different structures. In the one case, persons and groups are bound by traditions, conventions, and authorities, subjection to which is demanded by the conscience, which may be weak or strong, compromising or insistent, healthy or compulsory, reasonable or fanatic. Psychological or sociological explanations of such states of mind are fully justified. Nothing that happens in the mind should be exempt from psychological or sociological exploration and explanation. But within this structure of causation, another is manifest—what we might call the "structure of meaning" or, to use a famous medieval term revived by modern phenomenology, the structure of "intentionality" or the *noetic* structure (from *nous*, "mind"). This structure would be evident, for example, should a mathematician, psychologically and sociologically conditioned like everyone else, discover a new mathematical proposition. The validity of this proposition is independent of the series of conditions which made the discovery possible. In a similar way, the meaning of the unconditional in being and in what ought-to-be appears within the psychological and sociological processes which make its appearance possible. But its validity is not dependent on the structure in which it appears. Psychological and sociological pressures may provide occasion for the appearance of such structures; but they cannot produce the meaning of the unconditional. However strong the pressures be, they are themselves conditioned, and it is possible to contradict them and to be liberated from them, as, for example, from the father-image or from the socially produced conscience. This is not possible with regard to the unconditional character of the moral imperative. One can, of course, discard every particular content for the sake of another, but one cannot discard the moral imperative itself without the self-destruction of one's essential nature and one's eternal relationship. For these reasons, the attempts to undercut the unconditional character of the moral imperative by psychological and sociological arguments must fail.

There is, however, a more fundamental question, raised and thoroughly discussed by the ancient ethical philosophers, namely, the question of the moral aim. We have called it "becoming a person within a community of persons," and we have indicated that the centered person is the bearer of the spirit, its creativity, and its self-transcendence. Insofar as it is the moral aim to constitute and preserve the person with these potentialities, we can say that the moral imperative demands the actualization of man's created potentiality. But now the question arises: is this an unconditional demand? The answer depends on the idea of man's intrinsic aim, of the *telos* for which he is created. If the aim implies something above finitude and transitoriness, the fulfillment of this aim is infinitely significant, or unconditional in its seriousness. When Plato said that the *telos* of man is "to become as much as possible similar to the God," such a *telos* gives unconditional character to the moral imperative. If, however, the *telos* is, as in the hedonistic school, the greatest possible amount of pleasure to be derived from life, no unconditional imperative is at work, but merely the very much conditioned advice to calculate well what amount of pain must be suffered in order to attain to the greatest possible amount of pleasure. Between these two extremes of the definition of man's inner *telos* are several definitions which set a finite aim according to the formulation, but in which something unconditional with respect to the moral imperative shines through. This is true of utilitarianism, in which the moral imperative demands work for "the greatest happiness of the greatest number." Here pleasure is replaced by "happiness," and above all, it is not the individual happiness, but that of the many, which is the aim. And the happiness of the many is not possible without self-restraint in the individual's search for happiness. Therefore, a demand appears that cannot be derived from the merely natural trends of the individual, a demand that implies the acceptance of the other person as a person, and an unconditional element besides, whether acknowledged or not.

The Epicureans deal with the problems of the *telos* and the moral imperative from another angle. They also use the term "happiness," but for them happiness consists in the life of the spirit in community with friends, and in the creative participation in the cognitive and aesthetic values of their culture. The relationship to friends as well as to cultural creativity demands unconditional subjection to the norms and structures of friendship, knowledge, and beauty.

Nearest to Plato's definition of the human *telos* is Aristotle's thought that man's highest aim is participation in the eternal divine self-intuition. This state can be fully reached only by entering the eternal life above finite life. This does not mean that the individual has immortality but that, within time, he can participate in eternity through the "theoretical" life, the life of intuition. Wherever this state of participation is reached, there is *eudaimonia*, fulfillment under the guidance of a "good daimon," a half-divine power. To reach this goal is an unconditional imperative. And since the practical virtues are the precondition for fulfillment through participation in the divine, they also have unconditional validity.

We have used the Greek word *eudaimonia* (badly translated as "happiness") in order to point out the moral aim as described in several ethical schools. *Eudaimonia* belongs to those words that have suffered a marked deterioration in meaning. Most responsible for this process were the Stoic and Christian polemics against Epicureanism, which often unjustly confused Epicureanism with hedonism. The word in itself means fulfillment with divine help, and consequent happiness. This happiness does not exclude pleasure, but the pleasure is not the aim, nor is happiness itself the aim. It is the companion of fulfillment, reached together with it. If we derogate this concept of *eudaimonia*, we must also derogate the Christian hope for eternal blessedness. For, even though the Calvinist names the glory of God as the aim of his life, he experiences blessedness in fulfilling this aim and serving the glory of God. The same, of course, is true of *theosis* ("becoming Godlike"), *fruitio Dei* ("enjoying the intuition of the divine life"), or working for and participating in the "Kingdom of God" described as the aim of the individual man, of mankind, and the universe.

Happiness or blessedness as the emotional awareness of fulfillment is not in conflict with the unconditional, and therefore religious, character of the moral imperative. A conflict exists only when the function of self-transcendence in man's spirit is denied, and man is seen as totally imprisoned in his finitude. But this diminution of man to a finite process has rather rarely occurred in the history of thought. Even highly secularized philosophers were conscious of the function of self-transcendence in man's spirit, and consequently of the dimension of the unconditional or the religious dimension.

There are two concepts in the preceding discussion that have been frequently used without having been thoroughly discussed. The one is "conscience," the channel through which the unconditional character of the moral imperative is experienced, and the other is the term "religious" (in the title and in many other parts of this chapter). The concept of conscience will be fully discussed in Chapter IV. Regarding the concept of religion (which I have developed in much of my work), I can restrict myself to the following summary: the fundamental concept of religion is the state of being grasped by an ultimate concern, by an infinite interest, by something one takes unconditionally seriously. It is in view of this concept that we have formulated the main proposition of this chapter, namely, that there is a religious dimension in the moral imperative itself. Derived from the fundamental concept of religion is the traditional concept that religion is a particular expression, in symbols of thought and action, of such ultimate concern within a social group as, for example, a church. If the moral imperative were derived from religion in the traditional sense of the word, secular ethics would have to sever any ties with religion, for it rejects direct dependence on any particular religion. If, however, the religious element is intrinsic to the moral imperative, no conflict is necessary.

II

The Religious Source
of the Moral Demands

The first chapter avoided any detailed statement concerning the content of the moral imperative. It restricted itself to a discussion of the unconditional character of morality, whatever the moral demand might be, and however determined by historical and personal conditions. Its unconditional character was considered as its religious quality.

Undoubtedly the question of the ethical content—the question of what one must do—has already and persistently arisen in the minds of many readers. This question was not left totally unanswered; but the answer—that we must become what we essentially are, *persons*—is so formal that it does not offer any concrete advice. Yet such advice is necessary for the life of man. So also are principles, which are at the same time abstract and concrete, so that support for moral decisions can be derived from them. Are there such principles of moral action? If so, how can they be related to the ever changing conditions of existence? Is not ethical relativism the only possible answer, even in view of the unconditional character of the moral imperative?

The first problem of this chapter is to consider the positive aspects and the limitations of ethical relativism. For relativism is the predominant ethical theory and, in many respects, also a widespread moral practice. The facts that support this theory are obvious. The pronounced difference between primitive and modern ethics and between Western and Eastern, feudal and bourgeois, liberal-humanist and neo-collectivist morality, and the difference in ethical attitudes to the same event in the same locality by diverse social strata, diverse religious groups, and diverse generations strongly support ethical relativism.

For a certain time anthropologists dealing with primitive cultures were the champions of ethical relativism. Ever since the eighteenth century, anthropological research has shown a particular interest in the ethics of primitive man. His morality was supposed to demonstrate the conditioning of our own ethical ideas, whether feudal or bourgeois, Christian or humanist. Particular laws pertaining, for example, to killing, stealing, lying, and so forth, in one culture were compared with corresponding but different (and sometimes contradicting) laws in another culture, and the conclusion was drawn that there is no common ground in ethical thought among separated cultures. Ethics, according to this view, is culturally conditioned, and therefore ethics of different cultures are as different as the cultures themselves. In both cultural anthropology and popular understanding, such concepts are still widespread despite the fact that a sharp reaction has arisen against the primitive character of this method. We have learned (partly through the insight that a living reality is a structural unity, a *Gestalt,* and not a mechanical composite) that cultures are wholes, and that we cannot compare parts of them with parts of others, but must understand the significance of the particulars in the light of the whole. Then we may discover that the contrast of ethical demands in separated cultures is not a contradiction, but a different expression of a common fundamental principle. Ignorance of this insight has produced much naïve relativism in popular thought and unfortunately also among scholars when they unintentionally become philosophers. The method of structural analysis is a warning against a primitive use of the "primitives" in the argument for ethical relativism.

A positive and constructive criticism of the relativistic theories is embodied in the doctrine of the natural moral law. It is a very old, famous, and still rather vital theory that man by nature (in Christianity by creation) has an awareness of the universally valid moral norms. To every man this awareness is potentially given, even though actually distorted by culture, education, and his existential estrangement from his true being. This classical theory of natural law has only an indirect relation to the concept of physical laws, the laws of nature in the ordinary sense of the word. Natural law in our context is the law of moral reason or, as Kant calls it, "practical reason." For Stoic thought it has a common source with the physical laws in the divine *logos,* who is creatively present both in the laws of nature and in the natural moral laws of the human mind. Christianity accepted the Stoic doctrine, and most systems of religious thought have developed similar concepts. It is a general and unavoidable human problem, present in the quest for truth as well as in the demand for justice.

Its background is the awareness man has of the gap between what he essentially is, and therefore ought to be, and what he actually is, a consciousness of estrangement from and contradiction of his essential being. The emphasis on this estrangement by some radical Protestant thinkers has induced them to reject the theory of natural law completely. Man has totally lost what he essentially—or by creation—is. There is no knowledge of his true nature in him, unless it be given him by divine revelation. The revelation through man's created nature is veiled by his separation from God. A new revelatory experience is necessary, such as that which inspired the Mosaic law or the Sermon on the Mount.

But there is *self-deception* in every denial of the natural moral law. For those who deny it must admit that a divinely revealed moral law cannot contradict the divinely created human nature. It can only be a restatement of the law that is embodied in man's essential nature. And after having conceded this, these critics must go one step further toward affirming the doctrine of natural law. Man's essential nature cannot be lost as long as man is man. It can be distorted in the process of actualization, but it cannot disappear. The very statement that man is estranged from his created nature presupposes an experience of the abyss between what he essentially is and what he existentially is. Even a weak or misled conscience is still a conscience, namely, the silent voice of man's own essential nature, judging his actual being.

To defend the natural law theory against its religious critics is also to attack the nominalistic rejection of the idea of universal moral norms and its attempt to explain all ethical demands as expressions of social needs or of political power structures. If this were possible (which it is not), the concept of "man's essential nature" would have to be eliminated, and the experience of the conflict between what man essentially is and what he existentially is would have to be explained away. Undoubtedly, the concrete formulation of moral commands and their interpretation in ethical systems are largely conditioned by the social situation. But in all the varieties of cultures and religions and, consequently, of ethical systems, some basic norms appear. They are rooted in man's essential nature and ultimately in the structure of being itself. Their elaboration is the task of a developed theory of natural law. And here it might be added that such a theory underlies not only all ethical systems, but also all systems of "law" in the sense of jurisprudence.

The discussion of relativism has shown that basic ethical norms must unite an absolute element and a relative element. They must be universally valid and, at the same time, adaptable to the concrete situation. This tension appears conspicuously in the contrast between the Roman Catholic and a possible Protestant theory of natural law. The Roman Catholic theory asserts that it is possible to derive a considerable number of particular demands from certain universal principles through rational deduction. Such demands, if reached by sound methods of reasoning, are valid for all times and all situations. No revelatory event is necessary in order to discover them, and no change of the historical conditions can undercut their validity. There is, however, a point of uncertainty: those who analyze and deduce are human beings and, consequently, open to errors and distortions. Therefore, the church must decide what is the real natural law. Only the supranatural can confirm the validity of the natural, although the natural is true in itself. In this way the Catholic church has developed a system of natural moral laws which can be established and defended rationally, but which requires, because of human error, supranatural sanction by the church. The discussions regarding admissible methods of birth control or the educational authority of parents are actual examples.

Quite different is the Protestant attitude. Not much of a theory of natural law has been developed. This was partly due to the fact that Protestant biblicism attempted to derive ethical demands directly from the Bible, Calvinism particularly from the Old Testament. Another cause was the general Protestant distrust of reason, an implication of the doctrine of man's depravity in all parts of his nature, in mind as well as in body, in reason as well as in instincts. (The misleading term "total depravity" does not mean complete depravity, but estrangement from one's true being in *all* parts of one's actual being.) Finally, the Protestant principle denies that there can be any human institution, including a church with its doctrines and ethical demands, above the dynamics of history. A system of unchangeable laws of concrete morality contradicts the creative powers in life and spirit, and it contradicts the transforming work of the divine Spirit within and outside the church. Protestantism can accept the element of relativity in ethics and can develop with its help a dynamic doctrine of the natural moral law.

This, however, cannot be done without an answer to the question: is there a religious source of the moral demands? If so, how is it related to the formal answer given before, that the moral imperative demands that man become actually what he is essentially, a person within a community of persons? What does this mean concretely? What norms of moral action are implied in this demand? It will be necessary to answer these questions in sequence, and to build, step by step, a structure of moral action that embodies both the absolute and the relative, the static and the dynamic, the religious and the secular elements of ethical thought and moral experience.

First, let us examine the phrase "within a community of persons." Contemporary ethical theory has strongly emphasized the person-to-person encounter as the experiential root of morality. The decisive reason for this is the basic difference between the encounter of a person with another person and his encounter with nonpersonal realities (Martin Buber's ego-thou as opposed to ego-it). In the second case, man's encounter with nature outside him, for example, there is no limit in dealing with it. Man can make it into an object, dissect it, analyze it, or construct something new, a technical product, out of its parts or elements. Man can subject nature, progressively and almost limitlessly in all directions, to his knowledge and his action. The only limit is man's own finitude. But no one can actually establish this limit. Before it is reached nothing can resist man's cognitive and technical attack on nonpersonal reality. Nothing can resist man's will to transform it into an object and to use it for his purpose.

There is, however, a limit here and now in the ego-thou encounter. The limit is the other person. This seems a simple and obvious statement. But it is not so simple when we ask: where do we encounter a person? The answer—in every human being—is helpful only if we define living beings as human, if they are, according to their psychophysical structure, potential persons. This definition would include all degrees of the actualization of human potentiality, from the newborn child to the mature, wise man. But it does not determine which groups within the psychophysical species, human race, *have* the personal potential. Throughout human history this has been (and still is in some respects) undecided. Slaves, women, enemies, and special races were considered as objects with limited or unacknowledged humanity. And often children, the sick and old, the mentally abnormal and criminals were treated as mere objects, even though they belonged to a group whose personal potential was acknowledged, because they had not yet actualized or no longer were able to actualize their personal potential. This uncertainty with respect to beings who can be encountered as persons shows that the attempt to escape the relativities of history in the moral realm by formalizing the first principle cannot be successful. In the very moment the principle must be applied, traditions, conventions, and authorities, on the one hand, and criticism, decisions, and personal risk, on the other, determine the ethical demands.

Nevertheless, there are indications that man's essential nature makes itself heard in the midst of these uncertainties. Christianity, although it did not liberate slaves, gave them the status of potential persons by conceiving them as equal in their relation to God. And the Stoics, who achieved more than Christianity for political emancipation, did so in the name of the universal *logos* in which every human being participates. Both movements, and even earlier legislators who limited the arbitrary mistreatment of slaves, must have been aware of the fact that he who turns a human being (in the psychophysical sense) into a mere object suffers distortion of his own personal center. The same, of course, is true of the man who treats a woman as a mere object, or of a parent who deals with his child as though it were a thing, or of a tyrant who attempts to transform his subjects into tools for his purposes. They all become depersonalized themselves. Popular enlightenment in regard to these relationships has enlarged the circle of those considered potential persons. The circle in principle includes all human beings, although in reality it never does, even where the all-inclusive principle has been accepted, as, for example, in the racial conflict.

This discussion has led us to the deepest roots of what is usually called justice. All the implications of the idea of justice, especially the various forms of equality and liberty, are applications of the imperative to acknowledge every potential person as a person. Here, too, is the point at which every legal system of justice depends on some interpretation, consciously or unconsciously, of the moral idea of justice.

There is, however, a limit to the formulation of the moral principle of justice thus far. The acknowledgment of somebody as a person remains an external act that can be performed with legal detachment or cool objectivity. It can achieve justice without creating a relationship. Under many conditions this is the only way of actualizing justice, especially in encounters of social groups. But mere objectivity never occurs between human beings. Accompanying "pure" detachment is always an element of involvement. In the encounter of person with person within a community of persons, "community" also expresses involvement because it implies mutual participation, and, by participation, union. And the desire for union of the separated (which is ultimately re-union) is love. All communions are embodiments of love, the urge for participation in the other one. Justice is taken into love if the acknowledgment of the other person as person is not detached but involved. In this way, love becomes the ultimate moral principle, including justice and transcending it at the same time.

However, at this point it is necessary to combat several misinterpretations of the principle of love. First, it must be emphasized that if love takes justice into itself, justice is not diminished but enhanced. It has become creative justice in the sense of the Old and New Testament concepts of the *Yedaquah* and *Dikaiosyne* of God that both judges and saves. The frequent cry of Jews who have suffered immeasurable injustice through two millennia of church history—"We do not want love, we want justice"—is based on a misunderstanding of the biblical idea of love. Love, in the sense of *agape,* contains justice in itself as its unconditional element and as its weapon against its own sentimentalization. It is regrettable that Christianity has often concealed its unwillingness to do justice, or to fight for it, by setting off love against justice, and performing works of love in the sense of "charity" instead of battling for the removal of social injustice.

One of the reasons for this misunderstanding of love is the identification of love with emotion. Love, like every human experience, of course includes an emotional element, and this can in the case of love prove to be overwhelmingly strong. But this element is not the whole of love. Above all, love as *agape* is far removed from pity, although it can have elements of pity within a particular situation. Nietzsche's attack on the Christian idea of love is caused by this confusion. But it should serve to warn the Christian church to demonstrate in teaching, preaching, and liturgy the unconditional demand for justice in the very nature of *agape*. (I believe it would be salutary if the word "love" in the sense of *agape* could be avoided for a long time, and the word *agape* introduced into modern language.)

Agape is a quality of love, that quality which expresses the self-transcendence of the religious element in love. If love is the ultimate norm of all moral demands, its *agape* quality points to the transcendent source of the content of the moral imperative. For *agape* transcends the finite possibilities of man. Paul indicates this in his great hymn to love (I Corinthians 13) when he describes *agape* as the highest work of the divine Spirit, and as an element of the eternal life, even beyond faith and hope.

Agape as the self-transcending element of love is not separated from the other elements that usually are described as *epithymia*—the *libido* quality of love, *philia*—the friendship quality of love, and *eros*—the mystical quality of love. In all of them what we have called "the urge toward the reunion of the separated" is effective, and all of them stand under the judgment of *agape*. For love is one, even if one of its qualities predominates. None of the qualities is ever completely absent. There is, for example, the compassion element of *philia* and *eros* in *agape*, and there is the *agape* quality in genuine compassion (a fact important for the dialogue between Christianity and Buddhism). It is this *agape* element that prevents participation in the other one from becoming mere identification with him, as compassion prevents *agape* from becoming a detached act of mere obedience to the "law of love." And there is *eros* in *agape*, and *agape* in *eros*, a fact that permitted Christianity to receive into itself the *eros*-created classical culture, both rational and mystical. It is the *agape* element in *eros* that prevents culture from becoming a nonserious, merely transitory entertainment, just as *eros* prevents *agape* from becoming a moralistic turning away from the creative potentialities in nature and man toward an exclusive commitment to a God who can only be feared or obeyed, but not loved. For without *eros* toward the ultimate good there is no love toward God. Even the libidinous quality of love is always present in the highest forms of *eros, philia,* and *agape.* Man is a multidimensional unity and not a composite of parts.* Therefore, all elements of man's being participate in every moral decision and action.

On this basis we may judge asceticism in the light of the principle of *agape.* First, nothing created is bad in itself. Matter is not an antidivine principle from which the "soul" has to be liberated. The desire for union with material reality through the senses is an expression of love as *libido.* And in *libido,* elements of *eros, philia,* and *agape* are present, as *libido* is present in them. As in all other instances, the problem is how much *agape* is effective in the *libido* drives of love —in the desire for food, drink, sex, and aesthetic enjoyment. If the *libido* quality overpowers the *agape* element, and with it also the *eros* and *philia* elements, resistance in the name of *agape* is necessary and, under some conditions, partial or total asceticism with respect to things that are in themselves good. This "disciplinary" asceticism is quite different from the "ontological" asceticism which avoids things because of the material element in them. The former is affirmed by *agape,* the latter rejected by it.

This distinction applies also to the ecstatic element of religion which has a definite psychosomatic dimension in unity with its spiritual dimension. The union of these two factors characterizes every genuine ecstasy, including every serious prayer that reaches to the divine Presence. The *libido* element in love prevents *agape* from becoming a rational

* These ideas are fully elaborated in the first section of the third volume of my *Systematic Theology* (Chicago: University of Chicago Press, 1963), under the heading, "Life and the Spirit."

calculation of how to give the best possible help to others, as the *agape* element in love prevents *libido* from running wild and destroying the centered person, and with it the power of *eros* and *philia*.

Love is one. Its different qualities belong to each other, although they may become isolated and antagonistic toward each other. Decisive in all situations is *agape*, because it is united with justice and transcends the finite limits of human love. Therefore, in any conflict of the qualities of love, *agape* is the determining element. Only on this basis can love be called the ultimate source of moral demands. If love is understood in this way a second answer to the question of religion and morality is provided. The first was the unconditional character of the moral imperative. The second is the transcendent character of the ultimate source of moral demands— love under the dominance of *agape*. This again demonstrates that morality has a religious quality even when independent of any system of ethics that belongs to a religion in the narrower sense of the word.

In calling love the source of moral norms we have answered the first question of this chapter, namely, that of the relativity of ethics. For love is both absolute and relative by its very nature. An unchanging principle, it nevertheless always changes in its concrete application. It "listens" to the particular situation. Abstract justice cannot do this; but justice taken into love and becoming "creative justice" or *agape* can do so. *Agape* acts in relation to the concrete demands of the situation—its conditions, its possible consequences, the inner status of the people involved, their hidden motives, their limiting complexes, and their unconscious desires and anxieties. Love perceives all these—and more deeply the stronger the *agape* element is. (In line with this thought we might interject that the discovery of the psychology of the unconscious was a work not only of creative *eros*, but also of creative justice or *agape,* in spite of the antireligious bias of many representatives of the psychoanalytic movement.)

Christian theology has dealt with the problem of the concrete moral decision in terms of the doctrine of the divine Spirit. The "Spiritual Presence," the presence of the divine Ground of Being toward and in the human spirit, opens man's eyes and ears to the moral demand implicit in the concrete situation. Tables of laws can never wholly apply to the unique situation. This is true of the Ten Commandments as well as of the demands of the Sermon on the Mount and the moral prescriptions in the Epistles of Paul. "The letter kills" not only because it judges him who cannot fulfill the law, but because it suppresses the creative potentialities of the unique moment which never was before and never will come again. The Spirit, on the contrary, opens the mind to these potentialities and determines the decisions of love in a particular situation. In this way the problem of the absolute and the relative character of the moral demands is solved in principle. Love, as the ultimate principle of morality, is always the same. Love entering the unique situation, in the power of the Spirit, is always different. Therefore love liberates us from the bondage to absolute ethical traditions, to conventional morals, and to authorities that claim to know the right decision perhaps without having listened to the demand of the unique moment. The Spirit is the Spirit of newness. It breaks the prison of any absolute moral law, even when vested with the authority of a sacred tradition. Love can reject as well as utilize every moral tradition, and it always scrutinizes the validity of a moral convention. But love itself cannot question itself and it cannot be questioned by anything else.

The problem of this chapter—the religious source of the moral demands—has so far been answered in three statements concerning the ultimate principle of ethical norms. The first statement referred to the idea of justice, the affirmation of every person as a person. The second described love, taking justice into itself, as the ultimate principle of moral demands. And the third pointed to the dependence of moral demands on the concrete situation in its uniqueness.

There is, however, one unanswered question, namely, what is the function of the formulated laws for moral action? They appear abundantly in sacred texts that consecrate them and provide them with an almost unconditional validity. We must now ask: what is their significance within the structure developed up to this point? The answer lies in the word "wisdom." They represent the wisdom of the past about man, his relation to others and to himself, his predicament in temporal existence, and the *telos* or inner aim of his being. Wisdom, in the later centuries of the ancient world, became (like *logos*) a divine power, mediating between God and the world and between God and man. It was (again like *logos*) a principle of the divine self-manifestation in nature and history. According to the book of Job, God made the world while looking at "Wisdom" which was beside Him. In history it has inspired men and showed them the right way; it has had revelatory power and it became embodied in Jesus as the Christ. Wisdom, in this sense, is the source of the tables of laws in many religions and cultures. From the point of view of man, revelations, mediated by wisdom, are the result of both accumulated experience and revelatory visions. As such, they are of tremendous weight, but do not possess unconditional validity. They guide the conscience in concrete situations, but none of them, taken as law, has absolute validity. Even the Ten Commandments express not only man's essential nature but also the wisdom and the limitations of an early feudal culture. Certainly there is risk in deviating from the wisdom embodied in a concrete tradition. But there is also risk in accepting a tradition without questioning it. The former is an external and an internal risk, the latter only an internal risk. The former brings isolation and attack, the latter safety and praise. But accepting or trespassing traditional morals is spiritually justified only if done with self-scrutiny, often in the pain of a split conscience, and with the courage to decide even when the risk of error is involved. (See Chapter IV.)

Most human beings follow the guidance of the moral tradition when they obey the moral imperative. Everyone needs such guidance for his daily life and its innumerable large and small ethical questions. A considerable amount of moral habit is necessary in order to fulfill the demands of an average existence. Therefore, the tables of laws, which are commandments of the divine-human wisdom of all generations, are gifts of grace, although they can become destructive when elevated to absolute validity and substituted for *agape* and its power to listen to the voice of the "now."

One might ask: is love also the ultimate principle for social ethics? And we must answer affirmatively, because the encounter of social groups is an encounter in which reunion of the separated is the *telos,* just as it is in the person-to-person encounter. But there is a decisive difference. Social groups are power groups with no personal center. They have a changing organizational center in terms of their government. But they have no personal center. This means that there are great differences in the way love is effective in social ethics. Any attempt to identify the problems of personal ethics and social ethics (as does legalistic pacifism, for example) ignores the reality of power in the social realm, and so confuses the organizational centeredness of a historical group with the personal centeredness of a person. A discussion of the problems indicated by this statement requires the development of a philosophy of power. This we cannot do within the framework of the present study.*

To summarize the thesis of this chapter: the religious source of the moral demands is love under the domination of its *agape* quality, in unity with the imperative of justice to acknowledge every being with personal potential as a person, being guided by the divine-human wisdom embodied in the moral laws of the past, listening to the concrete situation, and acting courageously on the basis of these principles.

Out of such decisions in the power of love new insights would grow. And they might transform the given tables of laws into something more adequate for our situation as a whole as well as for innumerable individual situations. Should this occur, love as the ultimate principle of the moral demands would be powerfully vindicated.

---

* But I have developed such a philosophy in my volume *Love, Power and Justice.*

III

The Religious Element
in Moral Motivation

After having discovered its religious dimension in the unconditional character of the moral imperative, and the religious
source of the moral demands under the dominance of *agape,*
we now must ask whether there is a religious element in the
process of moral motivation.

The question leads immediately to the concept of law. The
unconditional moral imperative confronts us as the sacred
moral law. It appears as the only justifiable motivation. Any
other motivation would seem to introduce conditions that
violate the unconditional character of morality. This is the
basic point of view of Kant's rigoristic (not Puritan or Pietist)
ethical theory. It would reduce the religious element in
morality to the unconditional character of the moral imperative. We have already trespassed against this restriction
with respect to the source of the ethical demands by establishing love as this source, without surrendering the formal strict-
ness of the Kantian principles. We must now do likewise with
respect to moral motivation.

As the linguistic form itself indicates, the moral imperative
has the form of a commandment and, if generalized, a law.
We have discussed the term "law" in connection with the
natural laws of morals, and distinguished it from the physical
laws of nature. This difference extensively influences the

problem of moral motivation: the moral law is experienced as law only because man is estranged from the structural law of his essential being, namely, to become a centered person. This law belongs to him. It is his nature. And it would never become a commanding law if he did not try to break through it. But if he is estranged from it, if he contradicts it in his existence, it becomes law for him. And since all human beings share this predicament, they all stand under the law. And even love becomes law for them—"Thou shalt love . . ." If love determined our being, if it were a structural law with which we were one, it could not become a law that commands or an expression of the moral imperative. It would be an expression of our being, one with it, and not standing in opposition to it.

We can use this understanding of the law as a key to two biblical stories of great symbolic power—one, the temptation of Adam, and the other, the temptation of the Christ. In the story of the Fall, God forbids Adam to eat from the tree of knowledge (which is also power). We ask: why is this prohibition necessary? If Adam had been one with his true being, the negative command would not have been necessary. But as a man, he had the freedom to contradict his true being. In his condition of temptation he had not yet done so, but the tendency was in him, which means that he was already separated from the natural unity with God. The law appeared when the first symptoms of separation appeared, and the innocence of the created state of being in God was shaken. The law was a warning, a summoning back to original innocence. But by this very fact the innocence was no longer innocence. Neither was it guilt. It was on the boundary line of both, and the name of this boundary line is "desire."

This analysis of innocence, desire, and law can also be applied to one of the most problematic stories of the Gospels, the story of the temptations of Jesus. Some theologians deny the seriousness of the temptations; others affirm it, but are not aware of the consequences of their affirmation. In declaring with the New Testament and most classical theology the seriousness of the temptations of Jesus, we must acknowledge that they are expressions of his true humanity. They should have protected his image against the seemingly irrepressible Monophysitic trends in all Christian churches— that is, against the theological error strongly supported by popular piety, which is to see in Jesus *a* god, walking on earth. But if the temptations of Jesus are taken seriously, the question arises whether their seriousness presupposes a separation from that unity with God that determines his whole life and makes him the selected "Son." The question can be answered by reference to the Adam story. Serious temptation presupposes desire for that by which one is tempted. Jesus, like Adam, stood between innocence and guilt, on the boundary line of existence where the commanding law appears. And Jesus quotes commanding words from the Old Testament against Satan.

With this insight into the two different meanings of law, law as structure and law as the demand to actualize this structure, we approach the question: has the law in the second sense a motivating power for the fulfillment of the moral imperative and its concrete demands? The answer, like the answer to the question of the ultimate principle of the content of morality, must be developed along several levels. For it is complex, representing the profoundest tensions in religious experience and in the history of Christianity.

The general question is: can the commanding law, which presupposes the contrast between our essential and our actual being, motivate us to transform ourselves in the direction of reuniting the actual with the essential? The first logically consistent answer: it *cannot!* For the very existence of the commanding law is based on that split. The law (in the following sections used only in the sense of the commanding law) is an expression of man's estrangement from his true nature. How would it then be able to overcome this estrangement? This logically unavoidable answer is also the psychologically experienced answer: The command to be good does not make us good. It may indeed drive us toward evil!

Let us consider this answer in several realms of experience. Most contemporary is the psychotherapeutic discovery that the least effective way of treating a person under a destructive compulsion—alcoholism, for example—is to direct him in terms of a moral command, "Don't drink any more!" No psychoanalyst worthy of his profession would commit this destructive error. The law, as stated by the analyst, would produce a tremendous resistance in the patient, and justly so. The patient would withdraw to his freedom to contradict himself, even though he might then destroy himself. The patient, in this action, defends a decisive element in human freedom. Psychoanalysts who (according to the latest fashion) begin to moralize to their patients, however cautiously, should remember that it is precisely the pathological loss of power to respond to moral commands that makes these persons patients. Most analysts are still conscious of this, preserving one of the deepest insights of psychotherapy, namely, that the law cannot break compulsions, that the "thou shalt" does not liberate. Instead of encountering the law, the patient encounters acceptance on the part of the effective analyst. He is accepted in the state in which he is, and he is not told to change his state before becoming acceptable. In some cases, especially in pre-analytic counseling, the acceptance can express itself in a description by the counselor of how he himself was or still remains in a similar predicament, so that he ceases to be merely the subject, and the patient merely the object, in the healer-patient relationship.

One has accused psychotherapy of permissiveness. In particular cases this criticism is just—formerly, even more so. But so far as the method is concerned, this permissiveness is a result of a simple confusion between acceptance and permission. In the analytic situation there is neither command nor permission, but acceptance and healing. If the power of the compulsion is broken, a counseling exchange between the healer and the healed may take place, and the question may arise as to what the patient should do with his newly regained freedom. Only then should the problems of morality, its content, and its motivation come into focus, and the analyst may become a friend or a priest to the patient. But then the further question for both of them must be raised whether the moral law, appealing to their freedom, has motivating power, or whether it is powerless without a religious element in it— the religious element being an acceptance that transcends the psychotherapeutic distinction between the healer and healed.

Another relationship in which the question of the motivating power of the law is decisive is the educational one, first within the family, and then in the school and any other situation where an educational element is implied. There are many problems connected with the motivating power of the law in the educational realm. First, it is necessary to distinguish between demands based on authority and demands based on rationality. The distinction is rarely absolute because there is always authority behind educational demands; and this authority always claims to be rational. Nevertheless, it makes a great difference to the child, if he can understand a parental order as adequate to the situation, or if he feels it as a mere exercise of incomprehensible authority. In either case the child may resist. But in the first, the resistance is not rebellious; it is a primitive form of self-affirmation, weakened by a subconscious acknowledgment that the order was justified. Then the essential nature of the child is partly united with the content of the command, and to the degree to which it is united, the order proves not to be a strange law imposed by adult authority, but an expression of the demand of a practical situation, such as the necessary regulation of hours at home and in school. Therefore, it is of great importance to the educational process to help the child to understand the objective validity of the orders he receives.

If this is not accomplished, or if the orders themselves are more the expressions of willful authority than of the situation, the child is driven toward a genuine rebellion, and three things can happen: the rebellion may succeed and a creative independence develop; or the rebellion may succeed externally but fail internally, and rebelliousness as a character trait may result; or the rebellion may fail externally and internally, leaving a broken, submissive character. These examples show the problem of the law in a realm where it is almost daily experienced, and where parents, teachers, and even philosophers of education, have concluded that the law should be removed altogether and replaced by a kind of organized permissiveness. This, however, has led to consequences in which the "dialectics of the law" are patently manifest. After a certain time (usually in later adolescence), the majority of children become well-adapted conformists, albeit on a superficial level. Those among them who feel this superficiality as emptiness complain that they never had to face the law seriously and remained without guidance to their own essential nature and its potentialities. In view of this situation one must agree with the apostle who was most critical of the commanding law—Paul—that "the law is good," for it expresses the created goodness of man, which man must face because he is estranged from it.

The reference to Paul leads to the realm in which the problem of moral motivation and, consequently, of the motivating power of the law, has been experienced and discussed most thoroughly and most profoundly in religion and theology. It is not the general question of the religious element in the moral motivation that concerns us at this moment, but the attitude toward the law in some of the greatest religious men. Their experience is not restricted to religion in the narrower sense of the word, but is typical of human experience generally. There is no text in theology, philosophy, and psychology that deals more profoundly with the problem of the law than the seventh chapter of Paul's Letter to the Romans. He praises the law as "holy in itself" and the commandment as "holy and just and good." He calls it "spiritual." In his "inmost self" he "delights in the law of God," he is "subject to God's law as a rational being." Without the law he would "never have become acquainted with sin." This is one facet of Paul's evaluation of the law: the law is the expression of what man essentially is and therefore ought to be, but what he actually is *not,* as the law shows to him.

The other side of Paul's evaluation of the law is based on his experience that the law commands us to do the good that we cannot do because we are estranged from it and under a power that contradicts our true being: "Clearly, it is no longer I who am the agent, but sin that has its lodging in me." But the law does more than show us our essential nature and our estrangement from it. The law awakens the sleeping sin: "In the absence of law, sin is a dead thing"; "When the commandment came sin sprang to life"; "Through the commandment, sin became more sinful than ever." It is obvious that Paul does not consider the law as a power of moral motivation. He was, on the basis of his own experience, aware of the fact that the commanding law produces "all kinds of wrong desires," but does not motivate the conquest of these desires and the reunion of his actual will with his essential will: "What I do is the wrong which is against my will."

Paul's experience is independent of the religious framework in which it appears. A humanist with insight into his spiritual predicament could fully agree with it. Actually, however, and not by chance, the problem of the law as motivating power appeared again in its profundity and explosive power in the Protestant Reformation. All Reformers fought the idea that man's "good works," his fulfillment of the law, could be a contributing factor in salvation, or the acceptance of man by God. Not the fulfillment of commandments (which is impossible in the state of separation from God), but the acceptance of the message that we are accepted, is the motive of moral action. Nevertheless, the Reformers maintained a threefold use of the law—first, in its legal function as the principle of the postive law, the law of the nations; second, in its power to awaken our conscience to the fact that our actual existence contradicts our essential being, that we are estranged from ourselves; and third, in its function as a mirror of what is good and bad in Christian life. Luther denied and Calvin affirmed the third function of the law. But all the Reformers denied its power of moral motivation.

Again it was a personal experience, namely, that of Luther, that led to the rediscovery of Paul's experience and its theological implications. The depth to which Luther felt the ambiguity of the law emerges in expressions of hate, not only against the law itself, but also against the image of God who lays down a law nobody can fulfill and who punishes those who trespass against it. The shaking anxiety produced by this thought, and the hidden hatred against God, break out in Luther repeatedly, even in his later period. In such a state of mind, man is not able to recognize the law as the expression of his own essential being; he feels it as a strange and tyrannical command. But as with Paul, this is not Luther's sole evaluation of the law. The interpretation of the Ten Commandments in Luther's *Small Catechism* demonstrates that he is able to see in the law the right expression of man's relation to God and man in such a way that the right relation to God —love and fear—provides the moral motivation. Beyond this,

his interpretation indicates, as for every table of laws, a particular situation—in this case the paternalistic kind of rural society in which he lived. (Cf. Chapter II.)

The ambiguity of the commanding law, as experienced by Luther, was the decisive problem for the entire period of the Reformation. The emphasis was different in different Reformers, but the basic answer was the same. The enormous tension produced by this ambiguity, however, slowly receded, and Protestantism became to a large extent a religion of the law, doctrinal as well as moral.

All systems, determined by the law, whether religious or secular, are systems of compromise. This is true of groups as well as of individuals; and it is true of the great majority of human beings and human situations in all periods. This happens because the moral law becomes embodied in state law, conventional rules, and educational principles (with or without the support of a particular religion), and exercises motivating power through tradition, public opinion, personal habit, and the threats and promises connected with all of them. In this way the commanding law has the power to produce moral action in an institutionalized form. It is, generally speaking, what the Reformers called the "first use of the law," its power to produce "civil justice," since obedience to the laws makes the existence of society possible. From the point of view of the unconditional moral imperative, and love as the ultimate principle of moral commands, these methods of motivating moral action are compromises, unavoidable in view of the human predicament, but far removed from the true nature of the moral. This is true not only because of the universal human estrangement, the struggle between man's essential and existential nature, the ambiguity of good and evil in every life process, the mixture of moral and amoral motives in every moral act, but also because social institutions as well as personal habits have an almost irresistible tendency to perpetuate themselves in disregard of the demands of creative justice in a new situation or under unique conditions, both in the communal and in the individual life. To summarize: the law provides moral motivation if morality becomes a thread within a texture of premoral forces and motives.

To acknowledge this aspect of man's predicament is an act of humility, demanded by honest self-evaluation. But this demand is not fulfilled by most people. They evaluate their highly ambiguous moral achievements as sufficiently perfect, morally speaking; and there are even some who evaluate them as expressions of the nearly perfect or most perfect moral fulfillment. They consider themselves as "moral men," or as "men of good will," and look down on those who are "immoral men" or who at least do not belong to the selected group of the "men of good will." They do not see the ambiguity of their goodness and the mixture of their motives. They are not hypocritical, but self-assured in their high moral standing. They do not feel that they need forgiveness, either in Christian or in humanist terms. They defend the motivating power of the moral law, pointing to themselves as examples.

But some of these "moral men" and some of the "immoral men" are, at some point, grasped by the unconditional seriousness of the moral imperative, and they then recognize its deep opposition to them, even to the best qualities in them. This experience unites Paul the "righteous Pharisee," and Augustine the "sinner," and Luther the "ascetic monk." They took the moral imperative without compromise and without self-deception, and concluded that the "naked" moral law has no motivating power. They looked for something that had this power, and they found it in the religious element which they called "grace," a word that requires much interpretation to become an answer also for us.

But before discussing grace as the power of moral motivation, I should like to recall two concepts which belong together and represent the highest levels that Greek humanism reached in solving the question of moral motivation, and which remain decisive for the amalgamation of the moral with the cultural.

One is classically expressed by Socrates when he speaks of the knowing of the good, which creates the doing of the good. The question, of course, is: what kind of knowledge can create moral action? It is immediately clear that it cannot be the detached knowledge of prescientific or scientific inquiry, nor can it be the practical knowledge of the day-to-day handling of things and people, even if such knowledge is elevated to the level of technical expertise or psychological skill, for any of this can be used for the performance of the most anti-moral actions. (Our most flagrant modern example of this is the Nazi system.) Since we cannot assume, unlike some of his critics, that Socrates was cognizant of this danger, we must search for another kind of knowledge he might have had in mind. Perhaps we approximate it when we use the modern term "insight." If Socrates did mean "insight," he stands in line with his great predecessors—for example, Heraclitus and Parmenides. Heraclitus' attack against those who are "fools" is not a criticism of the unsophisticated, but of those not subject to the power of the *logos,* the universal law of things and mind, the source of the physical and moral laws. Those who are not grasped by the *logos* are fools, and he directs his prophetic-philosophical wrath against them. In this way he established the idea of the wise man who unites knowledge with personal involvement in the universal *logos,* an idea which became of immense practical significance in the humanist-religious philosophy of the Stoics. Wisdom became the leading virtue in the later ancient world, combining cognition and morality.

Knowledge of the character of wisdom cannot be considered

as functioning in one direction only, as the cause of moral action, because it is in itself partly a result of moral action. Since one must be good in order to be wise, goodness is not a consequence of wisdom. The Socratic assertion, therefore, that knowledge creates virtue must be interpreted as knowledge in which the whole person is involved (insight). That is, a cognitive act which is united with a moral act can cause further moral acts (and further cognition).

It is worthwhile to look, in addition to the Heraclitean-Stoic tradition, to that of Parmenides and the Gospel of John. In the philosophical poem about being and nonbeing, Parmenides describes the visionary experience in which the goddess of justice (!) opens his eyes to the true way of asking the ultimate questions. He derives his insight from a kind of revelatory act which takes away his blindness to the truth, and guides him not to a better method of research (although this is an important consequence of his insight), but to a way of life as a whole. In the Fourth Gospel we also find passages in which truth is being. Jesus says, "I *am* the truth." There are others which state that truth can be done, those who do the truth will recognize the truth. Here the gap between the cognitive and the moral is conquered, and again it is obvious that this kind of insight cannot precede the moral act and motivate it, since it is itself partly a moral act.

A modern analogy to these ideas is provided by the psychotherapeutic experience. It clearly shows the difference between detached knowledge and participating insight. No one is helped in his personal problems by a thorough knowledge of the psychoanalytic literature. On the contrary, the analyst knows that a patient who claims to have insight into his own pathological state on the basis of such knowledge deceives himself, and often sets up an almost insuperable resistance against gaining true insight about himself. Only he who enters the healing process with his whole being, cognitive as well as moral, and therefore with emotional attachment to the process and its different elements, has a chance of gaining healing. But this cannot occur without a "walk through hell," the suffering implicit in the awareness of the dark, ordinarily repressed elements in our being. Here also, the moral change is only partly an effect of insight, as insight itself is partly an effect of the moral will to be liberated.

There is another concept by which classical Greek humanism attempted to answer the question of moral motivation. It is the concept of *eros* as used by Plato. In the second chapter we defined it as the mystical quality of love. This description of *eros* depends both on Plato's use of the word in the *Symposium* and on the reintroduction of the word into Christian mysticism by Dionysios the Areopagite. *Eros* for Plato is a mediating power, elevating the human mind out of existential bondage into the realm of pure essences, and finally to the essence of all essences—the idea of the good that is, at the same time, the idea of the beautiful and the true. As in the other examples of Greek tradition, the moral and the cognitive are not separate. *Eros* provides both insight and moral motivation, and there is a third element, the aesthetic desire for the beautiful which is implied in the good. This goal can be attained by *eros* as a divine-human power that transcends the moral command without denying it. *Eros* is the transmoral motivation for moral action.

To be impelled by *eros* can also be described as being grasped by that toward which *eros* drives. And thus we return to the principle of love, as discussed in the second chapter. It is one of the qualities of love that concerns us here—the mystical, the drive toward reunion with essential being in everything, ultimately with the good as the principle of being and knowing (in Platonic terms). Love in all its qualities drives toward reunion. *Eros*, as distinct from *philia* and *libido,* drives toward reunion with things and persons in their essential goodness and with the good itself. For mystical theology, God and the good itself are identical; therefore the love toward the good itself is, in religious language, love toward God. This love can be symbolized in two ways: in Plato it is the divine-human power of *eros* that elevates the mind to the divine; and in Aristotle, it is the power of the divine that attracts every finite thing and produces by this attraction the movement of the stars, the universe, and the human mind.

According to both formulations it is not the moral impera-tive in its commanding majesty and strangeness that is morally motivating, but the driving or attracting power of that which is the goal of the moral command—the good. The Greeks were aware of the fact that the moral realm, in the sense of personal and communal justice, does not furnish moral motiva-tion unless it is understood as a station on the way to some-thing ultimate in being and meaning—the divine. And the aim of everything finite is to participate in the life of the divine. The moral stage is a station on the way, and the motivation for it depends on the motivation for the transmoral aim, the participation in the divine life, as Aristotle expresses it both rationally and symbolically. These are the forms in which Greek humanism and its ethical thought expressed, in mystical-religious terms, the transmoral motivation of morality.

Again I should like to point out a contemporary analogy in the realm of therapeutic psychology. The question is whether *libido* is unlimited in itself or only under the conditions of human estrangement. Our line of thought decides for the latter (as opposed to Freud and his doctrine of the essen-tial necessity of cultural uneasiness and the death-drive). The difference is that essential *libido* (toward food or sex, for example) is concretely directed to a particular object and is satisfied in the union with it, while existentially distorted *libido* is directed to the pleasure which may be derived from the relation to any encountered object. This drives existential *libido* boundlessly from object to object, while the essential *libido* is fulfilled if union with a particular object is achieved. This distinguishes the lover from the "Don Juan," and *agape*-directed *libido* from undirected *libido*. The moral imperative cannot be obeyed by a repression of *libido,* but only by the power of *agape* to control *libido* and to take it into itself as an element.

Eros is a divine-human power. It cannot be produced at will. It has the character of *charis, gratia,* "grace"—that which is given without prior merit and makes graceful him to whom it is given. It is useful to remember the origins of the word "grace," because it plays an immense role in Christian religion and theology, and its meaning and relevance have become incomprehensible for most contemporaries both inside and outside the church. Graces are divine gifts, independent of human merit, but dependent on the human readiness to receive them. And the readiness itself is the first gift of grace, which can be either preserved or lost.

Theology has distinguished between "common" grace that works in all realms of life and in all human relations, and the special grace bestowed upon those who are grasped by the new reality that has appeared in the Christ. In both respects, the problem of moral motivation is decisive. What common and special grace accomplish is to create a state of reunion in which the cleavage between our true and our actual being is fragmentarily overcome, and the rule of the commanding law is broken.

Where there is grace there is no command and no struggle to obey the command. This is true of all realms of life. He who has the grace of loving a thing, a task, a person, or an idea does not need to be asked to love, whatever quality of love may be predominant in his love. A reunion of something separated has already taken place, and with it a partial fulfillment of the moral imperative. As a gift of grace, it is not produced by one's will and one's endeavor. One simply receives it. In this sense we may say: there is grace in every reunion of being with being, insofar as it *is* reunion and not the misuse of the one by the other, insofar as justice is not violated.

Elements of grace permeate everyone's life. One could also call them healing powers that overcome the split between what we essentially are and what we actually are, and with this split the estrangement of life from life and the hidden or open hostility of life against life. Whenever elements of grace appear, the moral command is fulfilled. What was demanded, now is given. But what was given can be lost. And it will be lost, if one forgets that grace fulfills what the moral imperative demands, and that it affirms and does not replace the unconditional seriousness of morality. Therefore, as soon as grace is lost, the commanding law takes over and produces the painful experience of being unable to become what one could and should have become.

This suffering under the moral law finally drives us to the question of the meaning of our existence in the light of the unconditional moral command which cuts into our finite and estranged predicament. We feel that the many gifts of common grace do not suffice; we ask for a grace as unconditional as the moral imperative and as infinite as our failure to fulfill it. We ask for the religious element of moral motivation directly, after we have experienced its indirect effect as common grace in the different realms of life.

The Christian message is above all a message of grace. There is no religion without this element. The Old Testament, where the law plays such a decisive role, refers in every part to the divine covenant between God and the selected nation, and to the promises beyond all threats and judgments. We might cite similar examples from many other religions. But Christianity, particularly under the impact of the Protestant Reformation, has emphasized the idea of grace more than any other religion. The concept of grace in Christian thought contains a polarity between the element of forgiveness and the element of fulfillment. The former can be expressed as the forgiveness of sins or—in a paradoxical phrase—the acceptance of the unacceptable. The latter can be described as the gift of the Spirit or the infusion of love controlled by *agape*. The former conquers the pain of morally unfulfilled existence, and the latter grants the blessedness of an at least fragmentary fulfillment. Neither is possible without the other, for only he who is grasped by the Spirit can accept the tremendous paradox that he is accepted. Nothing is more difficult than to face one's image in the mirror of the law and to say "yes" to it in terms of "in spite of." It demands much grace to reach this state. And on the other hand, the fragmentary fulfillment through grace can bestow blessedness only if the paradox of forgiveness conquers the pain of missing fulfillment or of lost grace.

Here the skeptical question may arise as to whether the paradox of grace diminishes the power of moral motivation in those who accept that they are accepted, although unacceptable. It is a very old question, used against Paul as well as against Augustine, against Luther as well as against Calvin, and against the Reformation as a whole by the humanists and the evangelical radicals. It is a justified question insofar as it points to the possibility of converting the paradox of grace into a cover for lawlessness. But the question is not justified in principle, because it shows that one has not understood that the courage to accept the unacceptable is a work of grace, a creation of the Spiritual power. Only if the acceptance of the unacceptable is misunderstood as a merely intellectual act does it remain without moral motivating power. Orthodoxy (in contrast to the early Luther) is largely responsible for this intellectual distortion of the paradox of acceptance of the unacceptable and, consequently, for the attacks on the Pauline principles in the name of morality.

The question of moral motivation can be answered only transmorally. For the law demands, but cannot forgive; it judges, but cannot accept. Therefore, forgiveness and acceptance, the conditions of the fulfillment of the law, must come from something above the law, or more precisely, from something in which the split between our essential being and our existence is overcome and healing power has appeared. It is the center of the Christian message that this conquest took place in the Christ, in whom a new reality beyond the cleavage appeared. It is therefore a moralistic distortion of Christianity to interpret the so-called "teachings of Jesus" as another law, heavier than the law of Moses. His words (not his "teachings") point the way to the new reality in which the law is not abolished, but has ceased to be commanding.

The first three chapters of this volume have sought to demonstrate that the relation of religion and morality is not an external one, but that the religious dimension, source, and motivation are implicit in all morality, acknowledged or not. Morality does not depend on any concrete religion; it is religious in its very essence. The unconditional character of the moral imperative, love as the ultimate source of the moral commands, and grace as the power of moral motivation are the concepts through which the question of the relation of religion and morality is fundamentally answered.

IV

The Transmoral Conscience

In this chapter I shall discuss the transmoral conscience. The theologian Richard Rothe, in *Christian Ethics,* has made the suggestion that the word "conscience" be excluded from all scientific treatment of ethics, since its connotations are so manifold and contradictory that the term can no longer be usefully defined. If we look not only at the popular use of the word, with its complete lack of clarity, but also at its confused history, this desperate advice is understandable. Understandable as it may be, we should not follow it, for the word "conscience" points to a definite reality which, in spite of its complexity, can and must be described adequately. And the history of the idea of conscience, despite the bewildering variety of interpretations that it has produced, shows some clear types and definite trends.

The complexity of the phenomenon called "conscience" becomes apparent as soon as we look at the manifold problems it has given to human thought; man always and everywhere demonstrates something like a conscience, but its contents are subject to a continuous change. What is the relation between the form and the content of conscience? Conscience points to an objective structure of demands that make themselves perceivable through it, and represents, at the same time, the most subjective self-interpretation of personal life. What is the relation between the objective and the subjective sides of conscience? Conscience is an ethical concept, but it has a basic significance for religion. What is the relation between the ethical and the religious meaning of conscience? Conscience has many different functions; it is good or bad, commanding or warning, elevating or condemning, battling or indifferent. Which of these functions are basic, which derived? These questions refer only to the description of the phenomenon, not to its explanation or evaluation. They show its complex character and the reason for its confused history.

The concept of conscience is a creation of the Greek and Roman spirit. Wherever this spirit has been influential, notably in Christianity, conscience is a significant notion. The basic Greek word *syneidenai* ("knowing with," i.e., with oneself; "being witness of oneself") was common in popular language long before the philosophers utilized it. It described the act of observing oneself, often as judging oneself. In philosophical terminology it received the meaning of "self-consciousness" (for instance, in Stoicism, the derived substantives *syneidesis, synesis*). Philo of Alexandria, under the influence of the Old Testament, stressed the ethical self-observation in *syneidesis* and attributed to it the function of *elenchos,* that is, accusation and conviction. The Roman language, following the popular Greek usage, united the theoretical and practical emphasis, in the word *conscientia,* while philosophers like Cicero and Seneca admitted it to the ethical sphere and interpreted it as the trial of oneself, in accusation as well as in defense. In modern languages the theoretical and the practical aspects are usually expressed by different words. English distinguishes *consciousness* from *conscience;* German, *Bewusstsein* from *Gewissen;* French, *connaissance* from *conscience* (although the latter word is also used for the theoretical aspect).

The development of the reality as well as of the concept of conscience is connected with the breakdown of primitive conformism in a situation that forces the individual to face himself as such. In the sphere of an unbroken we-consciousness, no individual conscience can appear. Cultural phenomena such as Greek tragedy, with its emphasis on personal guilt and personal purification, or in later Judaism, the stress upon personal responsibility before God, prepared for the rise of conscience by creating a definite ego-consciousness. The self, says a modern philosopher, has been discovered by sin. The merely logical self-consciousness does not have such a power. Without practical knowledge about oneself, produced by the experience of law and guilt, no practical self-consciousness and no conscience could have developed. Predominantly theoretical types of mentality lack a mature self. Even Nietzsche, who attacks more passionately than anyone the judging conscience, derives the birth of the "inner man" from its appearance. In pointing to the subpersonal character of guilt and punishment in primitive cultures, he praises the discovery of the conscience as the elevation of mankind to a higher level. The fact that self and conscience are dependent on the experience of personal guilt explains the prevalence of the "bad conscience" in reality, literature, and theory. It supports the assertion that the uneasy, accusing, and judging conscience is the original phenomenon; that good conscience is only the absence of bad conscience; and that the demanding and warning conscience is only the anticipation of it. Since ego-self and conscience grow in mutual dependence, and since the self discovers itself in the experience of a split between what it is and what it ought to be, the basic character of the conscience—the conciousness of guilt—is obvious.

Shakespeare, in *King Richard III*, Act V, Scene 3, gives a classic expression of the relationship of individual self-consciousness, guilt, and conscience:

> Oh coward conscience, how dost thou afflict me! . . .
> What! do I fear myself? There's none else by.
> Richard loves Richard; that is, *I am I.*

> Is there a murderer here? No. Yes, I am.
> Then fly. What, from myself? Great reason why,
> Lest I revenge. What, *myself upon myself?*
> Alack, I love myself. Wherefore? For any good
> That I myself have done unto myself?
> O, no! alas, I rather hate myself. . . .
> My conscience hath a thousand several tongues,
> . . . crying all, Guilty! guilty.

In the next moment, however, Richard immerses himself in the we-consciousness of the battle, dismissing self and conscience:

> . . . conscience is a word that cowards use. . . .
> Our strong arms be our conscience, swords our law.
> March on, *join* bravely, let us to 't pell-mell;
> If not to heaven, then *hand in hand* to hell.

While the Old Testament describes the experience but not the notion of conscience (Adam, Cain, David, Job), the New Testament, especially Paul, has the word and the reality. Through the influence of Paul (who in this case, as in others, introduced elements of Hellenistic ethics into Christianity) conscience has become a common concept to the Christian nations, in their religious as well as secular periods.

Conscience, in the New Testament, has religious significance only indirectly. It has primarily an ethical meaning. The acceptance of the gospel, for instance, is not a demand of the conscience. It does not give laws, but it accuses and condemns him who has not fulfilled the law. Consequently, it is considered to be not a special quality of Christians but an element of human nature generally. In Romans 2:14—15, Paul expresses this very strongly: "When Gentiles who have no law obey instinctively the Law's requirements, they are a law to themselves, even though they have no law; they exhibit the effect of the Law written on their hearts, their conscience bears them witness, as their moral convictions accuse or, it may be, defend them" (Moffatt).

According to these words, the conscience witnesses to the law (either the Mosaic or the natural law), but it does not contain the law. Therefore its judgment can be wrong. Paul speaks of a "weak conscience" when describing the narrow and timid attitude of Christians who are afraid to buy meat in the market because it might have been used for sacrifices in pagan cults. Paul criticizes such attitudes. But he emphasizes that even an erring conscience must be obeyed, and he warns those who are strong in their conscience not to induce, by their example, those who are weak to do things that would give them an uneasy conscience. No higher estimation of the conscience as guide is possible. Paul does not say that we must follow it because it is right, but because disobedience to it means the loss of salvation (Romans 14). We can lose our salvation even when we do something objectively right, if we do it with an uneasy conscience. The unity and consistency of the moral personality are more important than its subjection to a truth that endangers this unity.

In principle, Christianity has always maintained the Pauline doctrine of conscience, the unconditional moral responsibility of the individual person. Aquinas and Luther agree on this point. Aquinas states that he must disobey the command of a superior to whom he has made a vow of obedience if the superior asks something against his conscience. And Luther's famous insistence, before the emperor in Worms, that it is not right to do something against the conscience (in this case to recant a theological insight) is based on the traditional Christian doctrine of conscience. But neither in Paul nor in Aquinas or Luther is the conscience a religious source. They all keep the authority of conscience within the ethical sphere. Luther's refusal to recant his doctrine of justification is an expression of his conscientiousness as a doctor of theology. He declares that he would recant if refuted by arguments

taken from Scripture or reason, the positive source and the
negative criterion of theology. But he does *not* say—as has
been often stated by liberal Protestants—that his conscience
is the *source* of his doctrine. There is no "religion of conscience" either in the New Testament or in classical Christianity before the sectarian movements of the Reformation
period.

In the New Testament the relation of the moral conscience to faith as the foundation of the religious life is
dealt with in only two connections. In Hebrews 9:9 ritual
religion is criticized because "gifts and sacrifices . . . cannot
possibly make the conscience of the worshiper perfect."
Therefore, the writer continues, "Let us draw near with a
true heart, in absolute assurance of faith, our hearts sprinkled
clean from a bad conscience." Only perfect salvation can give
the moral status from which a good conscience follows. But the
"assurance of faith" is not a matter of conscience. The other
link between faith and conscience is given in the criticism
of heresy. Heresy entails an unclean conscience because it
involves a moral distortion. In I Timothy 1:19 and 4:2
libertines and ascetics, both representatives of pagan dualistic
morals, are rejected. Against them the writer says: "Hold to
faith and a good conscience. Certain individuals have scouted
the good conscience and thus come to grief over their faith."
They are "seared in conscience." The judgment that one
cannot be a heretic with a good conscience has been accepted
by the church. The moral implications of heresy were always
emphasized, although not always rightly. Heresy is not an
error in judgment or a difference in experience, but a demonic
possession, splitting the moral self and producing a bad conscience. On this basis the church waged its war against the
heretics of all periods.

Scholasticism raised the question: according to what norms
does the conscience judge, and how are these norms recog-

nized by it? The answer was given in terms of the artificial (or distorted) word *synteresis*, i.e., a perfection of our reason that leads us toward the recognition of the good. It has immediate and infallible evidence, being a spark of the divine light in us, the uncreated light in the depth of the soul, as the Franciscans asserted; the created light of our intuitive intellect, as the Dominicans said. The basic principles given by the *synteresis* are: (1) The good must be done; the evil must be avoided. (2) Every being must live according to nature. (3) Every being strives toward happiness. Conscience is the practical judgment that applies these principles to the concrete situation. It is *syllogismus practicus*. We are obliged to follow our conscience whether the *syllogismus* is correct or not. We are, of course, responsible for not knowing the good. But we are not allowed to act against our conscience, even if it is objectively correct to do so. Man has an infallible knowledge of the moral principles, the natural law, through *synteresis;* but he has a conscience that is able to fall into error in every concrete decision.

In order to prevent dangerous errors, the authorities of the church give advice to the Christian, especially in connection with the confession in the sacrament of penance. *Summae de casibus conscientiae* (collections concerning cases of conscience) were given to the priests. In this way the conscience became more and more dependent on the authority of the church. The immediate knowledge of the good was denied to the layman. The Jesuits removed the *synteresis,* and with it any direct contact between God and man, replacing it by the ecclesiastical, and especially the Jesuit, adviser. But the adviser had the choice from among different authorities, since the opinion of each of them was equally probable. Heteronomy and probabilism destroyed the autonomous, self-assured conscience.

In spite of these distortions, the medieval development

performed a tremendous task in educating and refining the conscience of the European people generally, and the monastic and semimonastic groups in particular. The depth and breadth of bad conscience in the later Middle Ages is the result of this education and the soil for new interpretations of the meaning and functions of conscience.

Turning to the "sectarian" understanding of conscience, we find the Franciscan idea of the immediate knowledge of the natural law in the depth of the human soul. But two new elements supported and transformed this tradition: the so-called "German mysticism," with its emphasis on the divine spark in the human soul, and the "spiritual enthusiasm" awakened by the Reformation, with its emphasis on the individual possession of the Spirit. Thomas Muenzer and all his sectarian followers taught that the divine Spirit speaks to us out of the depth of our own soul. *We* are not speaking to ourselves, but God within us. "Out of the abyss of the heart which is from the living God," wrote Muenzer, we receive the truth if we are opened to it by suffering. Since the enthusiasts understood this divine voice within us in a very concrete sense, they identified it with the conscience. In this way conscience became a source of religious insight and not simply a judge of moral actions. The conscience as the expression of the inward light has a revealing character.

But the question arose immediately: what is the content of such a revelation through conscience? Luther asked Muenzer, and Cromwell asked Fox: what is the difference between practical reason and the inward light? Both of them could answer: the ecstatic character of the divine Spirit! But they could be asked again: what bearing has the ecstatic form of revelation on its content? And then the answer was difficult. Muenzer referred to practical decisions in his daily life, made under the inspiration of the Spirit; and Fox developed an ethics of unconditional honesty, bourgeois righteousness, and pacifism. It was easy to ask again whether reasonableness and obedience to the natural moral law could not produce the same results. The "revealing conscience" is a union of mysticism with moral rationality. But it does not reveal anything beyond biblical and genuine Christian tradition.

An important result arising from this transformation of the concept of conscience is the idea of tolerance and its victory in the liberal era. The quest for "freedom of conscience" does not refer to the concrete ethical decision, but to the religious authority of the inward light that expresses itself through the individual conscience. And since the inward light could hardly be distinguished from practical reason, freedom of conscience meant, actually, the freedom to follow one's autonomous reason, not only in ethics, but also in religion. The "religion of conscience" and the consequent idea of tolerance are not a result of the Reformation, but of sectarian spiritualism and mysticism.

The modern philosophical interpretation of conscience follows three main lines: an emotional-aesthetic line, an abstract-formalistic line, and a rational-idealistic line. Secularizing the sectarian belief in the revealing power of conscience, Shaftesbury interprets it as the emotional reaction to the harmony between self-relatedness and relatedness to others, in all beings and in the universe as a whole. The principle of ethical action is the balance between the effects of benevolence and the effects of selfishness as indicated by conscience. Conscience works better and more accurately, the more the taste for the universe and its harmony is developed. The educated conscience has a perfect ethical taste. Not harmony with the universe but sympathy with the other man is the basis of conscience, according to Hume and Adam Smith; we identify ourselves with the other man and take his approval or disapproval of our action as our own judgment. This, of course, presupposes a hidden harmony between individuals and the possibility of a mutual feeling of identification. It presupposes a universal principle of harmony in which individuals participate and which reveals itself to the conscience.

The emotional-harmonistic interpretation of conscience has often led to a replacement of ethical by aesthetic principles. The attitude of late aristocracy, high *bourgeoisie,* and bohemianism at the end of the last century was characterized by the elevation of good taste to be the ultimate judge in moral affairs, corresponding to the replacement of religion by the arts in these groups. It was an attempt to reach a transmoral conscience but it did not reach even a moral one, and it was swept away by the revolutionary morality and immorality of the twentieth century.

The second method of interpreting conscience philosophically is the abstract-formalistic one. It was most clearly stated by Kant, and it was introduced into theology by Ritschl. Kant wanted to maintain the unconditional character of the moral demand against all emotional relativism, against fear and pleasure motives, as well as against divine and human authorities. But in doing so he was driven to a complete formalism. Conscience is the consciousness of the "categorical [unconditional] imperative," but it is not the consciousness of a special content of this imperative. "Conscience is a consciousness which itself is a duty." It is a duty to have a conscience, to be conscientious. The content, according to Ritschl, is dependent on the special vocation, a special historical time and space. Only conscientiousness is always demanded. This corresponds to the Protestant, especially the Lutheran, evaluation of work. It is the expression of the activistic element of the *bourgeoisie* and is identical with the bourgeois adaptation to the technical and psychological demands of the economic system. Duty is what serves bourgeois production. This is the hidden meaning even of the philosophy of the "absolute ego" in Fichte, who describes conscience as the certainty of the pure duty that is independent of anything besides its transcendent freedom. In the moment when transcendent freedom comes down to action it is transformed into obedience to a well-calculated system of economic services. It is understandable that this loss of a concrete direction of conscientiousness paved the way for immoral contents when they were commanded, for instance, by a totalitarian state.

Against the aesthetic-emotional as well as the authoritarian form of determining the conscience, attempts were made in modern philosophy to have rationality and contents united. The most influential of these attempts is the common-sense theory of Thomas Reid and the Scottish school, i.e., the moral sense is common to everybody, being a natural endowment of human nature (like the *synteresis* of the scholastics). Decisive for practical ethics is Hutcheson's theory of the sense of benevolence toward others. This theory adequately expresses the reality of British (and to a degree, American) conformism and natural benevolence in a society where the converging tendencies still prevail over the diverging ones, and in which a secularized Christian morality is still dominant.

Another attempt to find rational contents for the conscience was made by Hegel. He distinguishes the formal and the true conscience. About the first he says, "Conscience is the infinite formal certainty of oneself—it expresses the absolute right of the subjective self-consciousness—namely, to know within and out of itself what law and duty are, and to acknowledge nothing except what it knows in this way as the good." But this subjectivity is fallible and may turn into error and guilt. Therefore, it needs content in order to become the true conscience. This content is the reality of family, society, and state. With the state (as the organization of historical reason) the formal conscience is transformed into the true conscience. It is a mistake to link these ideas historically to the totalitarian use of the state and the pagan distortion of conscience by

national socialism. Hegel was a rationalist, not a positivist. His
idea of the state unites Christian-conservative and bourgeois-
liberal elements. His famous, though rarely understood, idea
of the state as the "god on earth" is based on the identification
of the state with the church as the "body of Christ," expressed
in secular terms. The conscience that is determined by the
state in this sense is determined not by bureaucratic orders
but by the life of a half-religious, half-secular organism—
the counterpart of the Christian-rationalistic common sense
of the Anglo-Saxon society.

While the Scottish solution is largely dependent on the
social attitude of Western Christianity and Hegel's solution
on Lutheran Protestantism, the spirit of Catholicism has received a new philosophical expression in recent philosophical
developments, of which I take Max Scheler as a representative.
In his doctrine of conscience, Scheler opposes the popular
conception of conscience as the "voice of God." He calls this,
as well as the quest for "freedom of conscience," a principle of
chaos. Instead of freedom of conscience, he demands subjection
to authority as the only way of experiencing the intuitive
evidence for moral principles. It is impossible to reach such
evidence without personal experience, and it is impossible to
have such an experience without acting under the guidance
of an authority that is based on former experience. In this
respect, ethical (we could say "existential") experience is different from theoretical (i.e., "detached") experience. Although
this completely fits the situation of the Catholic, it is not
meant as the establishment of external authority. "All authority is concerned only with the good which is universally
evident, never with that which is individually evident."
Ethical authority is based on general ethical evidence. But does
such a general ethical evidence exist? Or is philosophical
ethics bound to be either general and abstract or to be concrete
and dependent on changing historical conditions? And if this

is the alternative, can the problem of conscience be answered at all in terms of *moral* conscience?

A conscience may be called "transmoral" if it judges not in obedience to a moral law, but according to its participation in a reality that transcends the sphere of moral commands. A transmoral conscience does not deny the moral realm, but is driven beyond it by the unbearable tensions of the sphere of law.

It was Luther who derived a new concept of conscience from the experience of justification through faith; neither Paul nor Augustine did so. Luther's experience grew out of the monastic scrutiny of conscience and the threat of the ultimate judgment, which he felt in its full depth and horror. Experiences like these he called *Anfechtungen,* that is, "tempting attacks," stemming from Satan as the tool of the divine wrath. These attacks are the most terrible thing a human being can experience. They create an incredible *Angst* ("dread"), a feeling of being enclosed in a narrow place from which there is no escape. (*Angst,* he rightly pointed out, is derived from *angustiae,* "narrows.") "Thou drivest me from the surface of the earth," he cries to God in despair, even in hate. Luther describes this situation in many different ways. He compares the horrified conscience that tries to flee and cannot escape, with a goose that, pursued by the wolf, does not use its wings, as ordinarily, but its feet, and is caught. Or he tells us how the moving of dry leaves frightens him as the expression of the wrath of God. His conscience confirms the divine wrath and judgment. God says to him, "Thou canst not judge differently about thyself." Such experiences are not dependent on special sins. The self, as such, is sinful before any act; it is separated from God, unwilling to love Him.

If in this way bad conscience is deepened into a state of absolute despair, it can be conquered only by the acceptance of God's self-sacrificing love as visible in the picture of Jesus as the Christ. God, so to speak, subjects Himself to the consequences of His wrath, taking them upon Himself, thus reestablishing unity with us. The sinner is accepted as just in spite of his sinfulness. The wrath of God does not frighten us any longer; a joyful conscience arises as much *above* the moral realm as the desperate conscience was *below* the moral realm. "Justification by grace," in Luther's sense, means the creation of a "transmoral" conscience. While God is the accuser in the *Anfechtung* and our heart tries to excuse itself, in the "justification" our heart accuses us and God defends us against ourselves. In psychological terms this means: insofar as we look at ourselves, we must experience a desperate conscience; insofar as we look at the power of a new creation beyond ourselves, we can attain a joyful conscience. Not because of our moral perfection, but in spite of our moral imperfection, we are fighting and triumphing on the side of God. As in Dürer's famous painting, "Knight, Death, and the Devil," the knight goes through the narrows in the attitude of victorious defiance of dread and temptation.

An analogy to this "triumphant conscience," as developed by Luther personally as well as theologically, appeared in the enthusiastic philosophy of Giordano Bruno. The moral conscience is overcome by the "heroic affect" toward the universe and the surrender to its infinity and inexhaustible creativity. Participation in the creativity of life universal liberates the moral conscience, the bad as well as the good. Man, standing in the center of being, is bound to transform life as it is into higher life. He takes upon himself the tragic consequences, connected with the destructive side of finite creativity, and must not try to escape them for the sake of a good moral conscience.

While in Bruno the transmoral conscience is based on a mystical naturalism, Nietzsche's transmoralism is a consequence of his dramatic-tragic naturalism. Nietzsche belongs to those empiricists who have tried to analyze the genesis of moral conscience in such a way that its autonomy is destroyed—Hobbes and Helvetius, on the ground of a materialistic metaphysics; Mandeville and Bentham, on the ground of a utilitarian psychology; Darwin and Freud, on the ground of an evolutionary naturalism—all have denied any objective validity to the voice of conscience, according to their rejection of any universal natural (rational) law. Nietzsche carried these ideas further, as the title and the content of *Genealogy of Morals* show. He says, "The bad conscience is a sickness, but it is a sickness as pregnancy is one." It is a creative sickness. Mankind had to be domesticated, and this has been done by its conquerors and ruling classes. It was in the interest of these classes to suppress by severe punishments the natural instincts of aggressiveness, will to power, destruction, cruelty, revolution. They succeeded in suppressing these trends. But they did not succeed in eradicating them. So the aggressive instincts became internalized and transformed into self-destructive tendencies. Man has turned against himself in self-punishment; he is separated from his animal past from which he had derived strength, joy, and creativity. But he cannot prevent his instincts from remaining alive. They require permanent acts of suppression, the result of which is the bad conscience, a great thing in man's evolution, an ugly thing if compared with man's real aim.

Nietzsche describes this aim in terms which remind one of Luther's descriptions of the transmoral conscience: "Once in a stronger period than our morbid, desperate present, he must appear, the man of the great love and the great contempt, the creative spirit who does now allow his driving strength to be turned to a transcendent world." Nietzsche calls him the man "who is strong through wars and victories, who needs conquest, adventure, danger, even pain." This man is "beyond good and evil" in the moral sense. At the same time, he is good in the metaphysical (or mystical) sense that he is in unity with life universal. He has a transmoral conscience, not on the basis of a paradoxical unity with God (such as Luther has), but on the basis of an enthusiastic unity with life in its creative and destructive power.

Recent "existential" philosophy has developed a doctrine of transmoral conscience that follows the general lines of Luther, Bruno, and Nietzsche. Heidegger, the main representative of existential philosophy, says, "The call of conscience has the character of the demand that man in his finitude actualize his genuine potentialities, and this means an appeal to become guilty." Conscience summons us to ourselves, calling us back from the talk of the market and the conventional behavior of the masses. It has no special demands; it speaks to us in the "mode of silence." It tells us only to act and to become guilty by acting, for every action is unscrupulous. He who acts experiences the call of conscience and, at the same time, has the experience of contradicting his conscience, of being guilty. "Existence as such is guilty." Only self-deception can give a good moral conscience, since it is impossible *not* to act and since every action implies guilt. We *must* act, and the attitude in which we *can* act is "resoluteness." Resoluteness transcends the moral conscience, its arguments and prohibitions. It determines a situation instead of being determined by it. *The good, transmoral conscience consists in the acceptance of the bad, moral conscience,* which is unavoidable whenever decisions are made and acts are performed.

The way from Luther's to Heidegger's idea of a transmoral conscience was a dangerous one. "Transmoral" can mean the re-establishment of morality from a point above morality, or it can mean the destruction of morality from a point below morality. The empiricists from Hobbes to Freud have analyzed moral conscience, but they have not destroyed it. Either they were dependent in their concrete ethics on Anglo-Saxon common sense; or they identified utility with the social conventions of a well-established *bourgeoisie;* or they cultivated a high sense of conscientiousnes, in scientific honesty as well as in the fulfillment of duties; or they did not dare, unconsciously or consciously, to draw the radical moral consequences of their dissolution of the conscience. In Nietzsche and Heidegger none of these inhibitions is left. But it is not without *some* justification that these names are connected with the antimoral movements of fascism or national socialism. Even Luther has been linked with them, as have Machiavelli and Bruno.

This raises the questions: is the idea of a transmoral conscience tenable? Or is it so dangerous that it cannot be maintained? But if the idea must be dismissed, religion as well as analytic psychotherapy would also have to be dismissed. For in both of them, the moral conscience is transcendent—in religion by the acceptance of the divine grace that breaks through the realm of law and creates a joyful conscience, and in depth psychology by the acceptance of one's own conflicts when looking at them and suffering under their ugliness without an attempt to suppress them and to hide them from oneself. Indeed, it is impossible *not* to transcend the moral conscience because it is impossible to unite a *sensitive* and a *good* conscience. Those who have a sensitive conscience cannot escape the question of the transmoral conscience. The moral conscience drives beyond the sphere in which it is valid to the sphere from which it must receive its conditional validity.

V
Ethics in a
Changing World

"Changing World" in the title of this chapter does not mean the general change implied in everything that exists. Neither does it mean the continuous change involved more fundamentally with history than with nature. But it points to the fact that we are living in a historical period, characterized by a radical and revolutionary transformation of one historical era into another. Nobody can doubt this fact seriously, and nobody who has even a minimum of historical understanding would do so after what has occurred during recent years. We are in the midst of a world revolution affecting every section of human existence, forcing upon us a new interpretation of life and the world.

What about ethics in this connection? Does it represent a realm above change? Is it suprahistorical in its foundation, its values, and its commands? Or does it follow the stream of historical becoming, and will it be transformed as rapidly as the other realms of life are transformed in our days? If the latter be true, what authority, what power of shaping human life remains in it? Can the unconditional claim with which every moral demand imposes itself on human conscience be maintained if the contents of the demand are different in every period of history? But if the former be the case—if ethics constitutes a realm above history, immovable and unconcerned by historical change—how can it influence man, living in history and transformed by history? Would it not remain a strange body within the context of human experience, separated from it in untouchable remoteness, perhaps worthy of awe but without actual influence on the life-process?

In order to answer these questions and to make them pertinent to our present situation, I intend to deal, first, with some solutions that have already appeared in the history of human thought, and are still of great actual importance; second, I wish to give my own solution; and, third, I will try to apply this solution to the present world-situation by giving some practical examples.

There are three great types of life and thought representing three different solutions of the problem of ethics in historical change: first, the static supranaturalistic solution, represented by the Roman Catholic church and expressed in the ethics of Thomas Aquinas; second, the dynamic-naturalistic solution, represented by the National Socialist movement and expressed in the ethics of the philosophers of life; third, the rationalistic-progressive solution, represented by Anglo-Saxon common sense and expressed in the ethics of the philosophers of reason.

With tremendous psychological power the static supranaturalistic solution maintains the eternal and immovable character of the ethical norms and commands. Philosophy and theology co-operate in this direction. The world is conceived as a system of eternal structures, preformed in the divine mind, which are substance and essence of everything and which establish the norms and laws for man's personal and social practice. Philosophy discovers these structures and laws, and revelation confirms and amends them. Revelation adds some superstructures of its own that are new and higher laws, but equally eternal and immovable. Both the natural and the supranatural structures together form a hierarchy of powers and values that control nature and are supposed to control human activities. The church, itself a hierarchical system, teaches this system, educates for it, fights for its political realization, and defends it against new systems. But in so doing the church cannot disregard the actual situation and historical changes. The church must adapt its ethical system to new problems and new demands. The Catholic church has been able to do just this, admirably, for centuries, and the living authority of the Pope is still a marvelous instrument for achieving adaptations without losing its immovable basis.

Nevertheless, it is obvious that the Catholic church did not fully succeed in dealing with the presuppositions and demands of the bourgeois era. Protestantism and the Enlightenment created new systems of ethics standing in opposition to the supposedly eternal system of the medieval church. And when the church tried to proceed with the stream of the rising *bourgeoisie,* as, for example, in the moral preachings of seventeenth- and eighteenth-century Jesuitism and in the teachings of nineteenth-century modernism, either it lost its seriousness and authority or it gave the unhappy impression of rearguard action in which every position is defended as long as possible and then surrendered. And the important utterances of the Holy See during the nineteenth century concerning social and political problems presuppose, in order to be applicable, the unbroken unity and authority of the Christian church, which no longer exist. Therefore, they did not at all influence the spirit of modern ethics and the direction of bourgeois society. The price paid by the static supranaturalistic answer to our question has been the loss of a determining influence on the changing world of the last centuries.

The opposite solution, represented by national socialism, was prepared for in two main ways—by the Continental vitalistic philosophy and by Anglo-American positivism and pragmatism, the latter being only a different form of the vitalistic philosophy. National Socialism has used and abused the philosophical motives of the Continental philosophy of life, especially of Nietzsche, Pareto, and Sorel. Philosophy must express life in its changing forms and trends. Truth, according to Nietzsche, is that lie which is useful for particular species of being. Values are produced and withdrawn in the dynamic process of life—biologically speaking, by the strongest kind of living beings; sociologically speaking, by the new élite; and politically speaking, by the eruptive violence of a revolutionary group. Change, being the chief character of life, is also the chief character of ethics. There are no independent norms above life, no criteria by which power can be judged, no standards for a good life. Good life is strong life, or violent life, or the life of a ruling aristocracy, or the life of conquering race. This implies that the individual, instead of being guided by the ethical norms that are manifest in his conscience, is obliged to merge his conscience with the group conscience. He must co-ordinate his standards with the group standards, as represented by the leaders of the group. The dynamic-naturalistic type of answer to the question of ethics in a changing world has a primitive-tribal character. It is, historically speaking, at the same time the most recent and the most ancient of all solutions of the ethical problem.

I have mentioned Anglo-Saxon positivism and pragmatism in this connection. It is an important task of this chapter to make it clear that pragmatism and vitalistic philosophy belong to the same type of ethical dynamism. When pragmatism speaks of experience, it surrenders the criteria of truth and the good no less than does vitalistic philosophy. There are for it no norms above the dynamic process of experience, that is, of experienced life. The question of what kind of life creates ethical experience and what the standards of a true ethical experience are is not answered and cannot be answered within the context of pragmatic thought. Therefore, the pragmatists and the positivists take their refuge in an ethical instinct, that is supposed to lead to an ethical common sense. This refuge is secure so long as there is a society with a strong common belief and conventional morals maintained by the leading groups of society. Such was the situation in the acme of the bourgeois development, for instance, in the Victorian era. But it was no longer effective when the harmony of a satisfied society slowly dissolved, and dissatisfied groups, masses, and nations asked for a new order of life. The ethical instinct of those groups was very different from the ethical instincts of the ascendant Victorian *bourgeoisie,* and the refuge in ethical instinct and common sense became ineffective. Pragmatism and positivism were unable to face this threat, because, in their basic ideas, they agree with the principles of the philosophy of life.

The intellectual defense of Anglo-Saxon civilization against fascist ideologies is extremely weak. Common-sense philosophy and pragmatism are not able to provide criteria against the dynamic irrationalism of the new movements; and they are not able to awaken the moral power of resistance necessary for the maintenance of the humanistic values embodied in Western and Anglo-Saxon civilization. It is not positivism and pragmatism, but the remnants of the rationalistic-progressive solution of the ethical problem on which the future of that civilization is based. The solution is the most natural one for undisturbed bourgeois thought and is still deeply rooted in the subconscious of contemporary philosophers as well as of laymen.

There are, according to this point of view, some eternal principles, the natural law of morals, but without the supranatural sanction claimed for it in the Catholic system. These principles, as embodied in the Bill of Rights, are like stars that always remain remote from every human realization but that, like stars, show the direction in which mankind must go. Once discovered, they cannot disappear again, although their theoretical and practical realization is always in process toward a higher perfection. In this way they are adaptable to every human situation.

Is this the solution of the problem of ethics in a changing world? In some ways it is, in some ways not. It indicates the direction in which the solution must be sought. There must be something immovable in the ethical principle, the criterion and standard of all ethical change. There must be a power of change within the ethical principle itself. And both must be united. But the rationalistic-progressive solution is far from reaching this unity. It establishes some principles, such as freedom and equality, in the name of the absolute natural law to be found in nature and human reason at any time and in any place. Mankind is supposed to realize these principles, theoretically and practically, in a process of approximation. It is the same natural law, the same principles that always have been more or less known, more or less received in reality. "More or less" points to a quantitative difference, not to a qualitative change, not to new creations in the ethical realm. Ethics in a changing world changes only quantitatively, that is, as far as progress or regression with respect to their realization is concerned. More or less freedom and more or less equality are admitted, but not a new freedom or a new equality.

But the principles on which the progressive-rationalistic solution is based represent a special pattern, a special type of freedom and equality, that of the later ancient and that of the modern bourgeois period. They do not represent principles comprehensive enough to embrace all periods and creative enough to bring new embodiments of themselves. They are not eternal enough to be ultimate principles and not temporal enough to fit a changing world. Therefore, as the Catholic system was not able to adapt itself seriously to the modern period of bourgeois growth, so the bourgeois-progressive rationalism was not able to face the breakdown of the bourgeois world. Supranatural and rational absolutism in ethics both proved to be unable to adapt themselves to a fundamental change in the historical situation.

Is there a possible solution beyond the alternative of an absolutism that breaks down in every radical change of history and a relativism that makes change itself the ultimate principle? I believe that there is, and I think it is implied in the basis of Christian ethics, namely, in the principle of love in the sense of the Greek word *agape*. This is not said in terms of an apology for Christianity, but under the impetus of the actual problem in our present world-situation. Love, *agape*, offers a principle of ethics that maintains an eternal, unchangeable element, but makes its realization dependent on continuous acts of a creative intuition. Love is above law, and also above the natural law in Stoicism and the supranatural law in Catholicism. We *can* express it as a law; we can say as Jesus and the apostles did, "Thou shalt love." But in doing so, we know that this is a paradoxical way of speaking, indicating that the ultimate principle of ethics, which, on the one hand, is an unconditional command, is, on the other hand, the power breaking through all commands. And just this ambiguous character of love enables it to be the solution of the question of ethics in a changing world.

If we look at the principles of natural law as embodied in the Bill of Rights, we will discover that, taken as the concrete embodiments of the principle of love in a special situation, they are great and true and powerful; they represent love by establishing freedom and equal rights against willfulness and suppression and the destruction of the dignity of human beings. But, taken as eternal laws and applied legalistically to different situations—for example, the early Middle Ages, or the decay and transformation of economic capitalism—these principles become bad ideologies used for the maintenance of decaying institutions and powers. This is why Paul and Luther struggled so profoundly against the "Law," and why they insisted on the deadening consequences of the law and the vivifying power of love. *Love alone can transform itself according to the concrete demands of every individual and social situation without losing its eternity and dignity and unconditional validity.* Love can adapt itself to every phase of a changing world.

I should like to introduce at this point another Greek word, *kairos,* "the right time." This word, used in everyday Greek, received an emphatic meaning in the language of the New Testament, designating the fulfillment of time in the appearance of the Christ. It has been reinterpreted by German religious socialism in the sense of a special gift and a special task, breaking from eternity into history at a special time. *Kairos* in this sense is the historical moment when something new, eternally important, manifests itself in temporal forms, in the potentialities and tasks of a special period. It is the power of the prophetic spirit in all periods of history to pronounce the coming of such a *kairos,* to discover its meaning, and to express the criticism of what is given and the hope for what is to come.

All great changes in history are accompanied by a strong consciousness of a *kairos* at hand. Therefore, ethics in a changing world must be understood as ethics of the *kairos.* The answer to the demand for ethics in a changing world is ethics determined by the *kairos.* But only love is able to appear in every *kairos.* Law is not able, because law is the attempt to impose what belonged to a special time on all times. An ideal that appeared at the right time and was valid for this time is now considered to be the ideal for history as a whole, as that form of life in which history shall find its end. The outcome of this attitude is inevitably disillusionment and the rise of ethical libertarianism and relativism. This is the point at which the dynamic-naturalistic solution, despite its destructive consequences, was in the right, and still battles rightly against Catholic and bourgeois ethics. Or, expressed in terms of church history, this is the point at which Luther was right in his opposition to Aquinas and Calvin. Love, realizing itself from *kairos* to *kairos,* creates an ethics that is beyond the alternatives of absolute and relative ethics.

This solution can be clarified by some concrete examples. Let us consider the idea of equality, one of the foundations of rationalistic-progressive ethics. In the light of the principle of love, and in the perspective of the idea of *kairos,* the following can be said: love implies equality in some respect. He who loves and he who is loved are equal to each other insofar as they are worthy of love, the one for the other. However, nothing but precisely this principle of equality is implied— *essentially* implied—in love. Everything else is a historical embodiment of that principle in different situations, with love and the distortion of love at the same time. Looking at a Greek city-state, we discover that there is a political equality among individuals in a special group, and to a certain extent among all those who are free; but there is an absolute inequality between the free and the slave. Love is not manifest as *the* principle; but since it is potentially the principle, it is effective even in the religion and culture of Apollo and Dionysus. It is effective in the kind of equality that the city-state gives to those who belong to it, excluding slaves and barbarians. Love is effective even in this restricted equality, but it is a restricted, distorted love—love within the boundaries of national pride and racial discrimination. The central *kairos* in which love becomes manifest as what it really is has not yet appeared.

Nor did it appear in the period of the universal Roman empire, when Stoicism extended equality to all human beings

—men and women, children and slaves. Here the principle of love broke through the limitations of national and social arrogance, but it did so as a universal, rational law, and not as love. Stoic equality is universal, but cool and abstract, without the warmth and the communal element of the limited equality in the city-state. At its best, it is participation in Roman citizenship and implies the possibility of a man's becoming wise. In the Christian message, love becomes manifest in its universality, and, at the same time, in its concreteness: the "neighbor" is the immediate object of love, and everyone can become "neighbor." All inequalities between men are overcome insofar as men are potential children of God. But this did not lead Christianity to the Stoic idea of equality. Not even the inequality between lord and slave was attacked, except in the realm of the Christian community. Later, not the totalitarian but the hierarchical principle was supported by the Christian church in accord with late ancient and medieval society. The social and psychological inequalities of the feudal order did not seem to contradict the element of equality implied in the principle of love. On the contrary, the mutual interpendence of all the degrees of the hierarchy, the solidarity of all the members of a medieval city, and the patriarchalistic care of the feudal lords for the "people," were considered the highest form of equality demanded by the principle of love.

In bourgeois liberalism, equality was again interpreted in terms of the general natural law, the law of reason and humanity. Equality became equality before the law and the demand for equal economic opportunities. This was in accord with the principle of love over against the tyranny and injustice into which the older system had developed. But in the measure by which the equal opportunity of everybody became a mere ideology to cover the exclusive opportunity of a few,

the liberal idea of equality became a contradiction of love. A
new idea of equality arose, conceiving the equal security of
everyone, even at the sacrifice of much political equality. One
must not condemn the collectivistic and authoritarian forms
of equality just because they negate equality's liberal and democratic forms. Love may demand a transformation in this *kairos*.
A new creative realization of the element of equality as implied in the principle of love may be brought about in our
period. It will be good insofar as it is in better accord with
the demands of love in our special situation than were the
feudal and liberal forms. It will be bad insofar as it will become a distortion and contradiction of love. For love is eternal,
although it creates something new in each *kairos*.

I could refer to many other ethical problems in order
to demonstrate their double dependence on the principle
of love, on the one hand, and on the changing *kairos*, on the
other. For example, I could point to the evaluation of work
and activism in the different periods of history and their relation to leisure and meditation. It is obvious that a coming
collectivism will reduce the emphasis on work and activism
considerably by restraining the principle of competition. As
the struggle against some forms of feudal and ecclesiastical
leisure and meditative life was a demand for love in the period
of the decaying Middle Ages, and occurred at the time when
mankind began to control nature, so it is now a demand of
love and *kairos* that leisure and meditation return in terms
of a new more collectivistic structure of society over against
a self-destructive adoration of work and activism.

Other examples are the problems of asceticism and wordli-
ness, of self-control and self-expression, of discipline and
creativity, in their relation to each other. Both sides of
these contrasts follow from the principle of love. The negation of the first aspect would prevent the self-surrender implied in love; the negation of the second would destroy any

subject worthy of love. It depends on the *kairos* as to which of these aspects, in which form and in which balance with the other, is emphasized. For our present stage, neither the supranatural asceticism of the Catholic system nor the rational self-control of bourgeois society, nor the naturalistic war-and-state discipline of fascism can provide the solution. And the same is true of feudal eroticism, of bourgeois aestheticism, and of the fascist idolatry of vitality. Another solution is demanded by love and by *kairos.*

Psychoanalysis provides some elements of the solution, although mere psychotherapeutic psychology is not able to create by itself a new system of ethics. Other elements of the solution are suggested by the rediscovery of the classical meaning of *eros,* and by the different attempts to relate it to *agape.* Educational movements and criticism of the bourgeois ideal of the family have contributed a great deal. But everything is in motion, and the criterion of the final solution is the measure by which *eros,* on the one hand, and self-control, on the other, are shaped by love.

A final question must be answered. If love is the principle of ethics, and if *kairos* is the manner of its embodiment in concrete contents, how can a permanent uncertainty, a continous criticism which destroys the seriousness of the ethical demand, be avoided? Is not law and are not institutions necessary in order to maintain the actual ethical process? Indeed, law and institutions are required. They are required by love itself. For every individual, even the most creative, needs given structures that embody the experience and wisdom of the past, that liberate him from the necessity of having to make innumerable decisions on his own, and that show him a meaningful way to act in most situations. On this point Catholicism was superior in love both to Protestantism and to liberalism. And this is the reason why the younger generation in many countries eagerly demands laws and institutions to relieve them of their unbearable burden of having to make continuous ultimate decisions. No system of ethics can ever become an actual power without laws and institutions. Luther, in his great emphasis on the creativity of love, forgot this necessity. This is one of the reasons why the moral education of the masses in Germany is less thorough than in the Calvinistic countries. On the other hand, there is a greater readiness for a *kairos* in Germany than there is in the more thoroughly educated and normalized Western nations. Love demands laws and institutions, but love is always able to break through them in a new *kairos,* and to create new laws and new systems of ethics.

I have not mentioned the word "justice" in this chapter. It would be misleading in the present discussion because it is generally understood in the sense of the abstract natural law of Stoicism and rationalism. As such, it is either empty or is the concrete law of a special period, and is thus without universal validity. If justice is taken concretely, it means the laws and institutions in which love is embodied in a special situation. The Platonic ideal of justice was the concrete harmony of the city-state. In Israel, justice was the pious obedience to the commands of God. In medieval feudalism, it was the form of mutual responsibility of all levels of the hierarchy to each other. The liberal idea of justice was the abolition of formal privileges and the introduction of legal equality. In the more collectivistic society of the future, justice will be the system of laws and forms by which a sufficient security of the whole, and of all members, will be developed and maintained. It follows, then, that justice is the secondary and derived principle, while love, actualized from *kairos* to *kairos,* is the creative and basic principle.

I have given no definition of love. This is impossible because there is no higher principle by which it can be defined.

It is life itself in its actual unity. The forms and structures in which love embodies itself are the forms and structures in which life is possible, in which life overcomes its self-destructive forces. And this is the meaning of ethics: the expression of the ways in which love embodies itself, and life is maintained and saved.

RELIGIOUS PERSPECTIVES
Its Meaning and Purpose

This is a reprint of Volume IX of the RELIGIOUS PERSPECTIVES SERIES, which the present writer has planned and edited in collaboration with a Board of Editors consisting of W. H. AUDEN, KARL BARTH, MARTIN C. D'ARCY, CHRISTOPHER DAWSON, C. H. DODD, MIRCEA ELIADE, MUHAMMAD ZAFRULLA KHAN, ALEXANDRE KOYRÉ, JACQUES MARITAIN, JAMES MUILENBURG, SARVEPALLI RADHAKRISHNAN, GERSHOM SCHOLEM, D. T. SUZUKI, PAUL TILLICH.

RELIGIOUS PERSPECTIVES represents a quest for the rediscovery of man. It constitutes an effort to define man's search for the essence of being in order that he may have a knowledge of goals. It is an endeavor to show that there is no possibility of achieving an understanding of man's total nature on the basis of phenomena known by the analytical method alone. It hopes to point to the false antinomy between revelation and reason, faith and knowledge, grace and nature, courage and anxiety. Mathematics, physics, philosophy, biology and religion, in spite of their almost complete independence, have begun to sense their interrelatedness and to become aware of that mode of cognition which teaches that "the light is not without but within me, and I myself am the light."

Modern man is threatened by a world created by himself. He is faced with the conversion of mind to naturalism, a dogmatic secularism and an opposition to a belief in the transcendent. He begins to see, however, that the universe is given not as one existing and one perceived but as the unity of subject and object; that the barrier between them cannot be said to have been dissolved as the result of recent experience in the physical sciences, since this barrier has never existed. Confronted with the question of meaning, he is summoned to rediscover and scrutinize the immutable and the permanent which constitute the dynamic, unifying aspect of life as well as the principle of differentiation; to

97

reconcile identity and diversity, immutability and unrest. He begins to recognize that just as every person descends by his particular path, so he is able to ascend, and this ascent aims at a return to the source of creation, an inward home from which he has become estranged.

It is the hope of RELIGIOUS PERSPECTIVES that the rediscovery of man will point the way to the rediscovery of God. To this end a rediscovery of first principles should constitute part of the quest. These principles, not to be superseded by new discoveries, are not those of historical worlds that come to be and perish. They are to be sought in the heart and spirit of man, and no interpretation of a merely historical or scientific universe can guide the search. RELIGIOUS PERSPECTIVES attempts not only to ask dispassionately what the nature of God is, but also to restore to human life at least the hypothesis of God and the symbols that relate to him. It endeavors to show that man is faced with the metaphysical question of the truth of religion while he encounters the empirical question of its effects on the life of humanity and its meaning for society. Religion is here distinguished from theology and its doctrinal forms and is intended to denote the feelings, aspirations and acts of men, as they relate to total reality.

RELIGIOUS PERSPECTIVES is nourished by the spiritual and intellectual energy of world thought, by those religious and ethical leaders who are not merely spectators but scholars deeply involved in the critical problems common to all religions. These thinkers recognize that human morality and human ideals thrive only when set in a context of a transcendent attitude toward religion and that by pointing to the ground of identity and the common nature of being in the religious experience of man, the essential nature of religion may be defined. Thus, they are committed to re-evaluate the meaning of everlastingness, an experience which has been lost and which is the content of that *visio Dei* constituting the structure of all religions. It is the many absorbed everlastingly into the ultimate unity, a unity subsuming what Whitehead calls the fluency of God and the everlastingness of passing experience.

These volumes will seek to show that the unity of which we speak consists in a certitude emanating from the nature of man who seeks God and the nature of God who seeks man. Such certitude bathes in an intuitive act of cognition, participating in the divine essence and is related to the natural spirituality of intelligence. This is not by any means to say that there is an equivalence of all faiths in the traditional religions of human history. It is, however, to emphasize the distinction between the spiritual and the temporal which all religions acknowledge. For duration of thought is composed of instants superior to time, and is an intuition of the permanence of existence and its metahistorical reality. In fact, the symbol* itself found on cover and jacket of each volume of RELIGIOUS PERSPECTIVES is the visible sign or representation of the essence, immediacy and timelessness of religious experience; the one immutable center, which may be analogically related to Being in pure act, moving with centrifugal and ecumenical necessity outward into the manifold modes, yet simultaneously, with dynamic centripetal power and with full intentional energy returning to the source. Through the very diversity of its authors, the Series will show that the basic and poignant concern of every faith is to point to, and overcome the crisis in our apocalyptic epoch—the crisis of man's separation from man and of man's separation from God—the failure of love. The authors will endeavor, moreover, to illustrate the truth that the human heart is able, and even yearns, to go to the very lengths of God; that the darkness and cold, the frozen spiritual misery of recent time, are breaking, cracking and beginning to move, yielding to efforts to overcome spiritual muteness and moral paralysis. In this way, it is hoped, the immediacy of pain and sorrow, the primacy of tragedy and suffering in human life, may be transmuted into a spiritual and moral triumph.

RELIGIOUS PERSPECTIVES is therefore an effort to explore the *meaning* of God, an exploration which constitutes an aspect of man's intrinsic nature, part of his ontological substance. The Series grows out of an abiding concern that in spite of the release of man's creative energy which science has in part accomplished, this very science has overturned the essential order

---

*From the original design by Leo Katz.

of nature. Shrewd as man's calculations have become concerning
his means, his choice of ends which was formerly correlated with
belief in God, with absolute criteria of conduct, has become
witless. God is not to be treated as an exception to metaphysical
principles, invoked to prevent their collapse. He is rather their
chief exemplification, the source of all potentiality. The personal
reality of freedom and providence, of will and conscience, may
demonstrate that "he who knows" commands a depth of consciousness inaccessible to the profane man, and is capable of that
transfiguration which prevents the twisting of all good to ig-
nominy. This religious content of experience is not within the
province of science to bestow; it corrects the error of treating
the scientific account as if it were itself metaphysical or religious;
it challenges the tendency to make a religion of science—or a
science of religion—a dogmatic act which destroys the moral
dynamic of man. Indeed, many men of science are confronted
with unexpected implications of their own thought and are beginning to accept, for instance, the trans-spatial nature of events
within spatial matter.

RELIGIOUS PERSPECTIVES attempts to show the fallacy of the
apparent irrelevance of God in history. The Series submits that
no convincing image of man can arise, in spite of the many ways
in which human thought has tried to reach it, without a philosophy of human nature and human freedom which does not exclude God. This image of *Homo cum Deo* implies the highest
conceivable freedom, the freedom to step into the very fabric of
the universe, a new formula for man's collaboration with the
creative process and the only one which is able to protect man
from the terror of existence. This image implies further that the
mind and conscience are capable of making genuine discrimi-
nations and thereby may reconcile the serious tensions between
the secular and religious, the profane and sacred. The idea of the
sacred lies in what it *is,* timeless existence. By emphasizing timeless existence against reason as a reality, we are liberated, in our
communion with the eternal, from the otherwise unbreakable
rule of "before and after." Then we are able to admit that all
forms, all symbols in religions, by their negation of error and

their affirmation of the actuality of truth, make it possible to experience that *knowing* which is above knowledge, and that dynamic passage of the universe to unending unity.

The volumes in this Series will seek to challenge the crisis which separates, to make reasonable a religion that binds and to present the numinous reality within the experience of man. Insofar as the Series succeeds in this quest, it will direct mankind toward a reality that is eternal and away from a preoccupation with that which is illusory and ephemeral.

For man is now confronted with his burden and his greatness: "He calleth to me, Watchman, what of the night? Watchman, what of the night?"[1] Perhaps the anguish in the human soul may be assuaged by the answer, by the *assimilation* of the person in God: "The morning cometh, and also the night: if ye will inquire, inquire ye: return, come."[2]

RUTH NANDA ANSHEN

New York, 1960

[1] Isaiah 21:11.
[2] *Ibid.*, 21:12.

Revised December, 1966

harper ✦ torchbooks

HUMANITIES AND SOCIAL SCIENCES

American Studies: General

THOMAS C. COCHRAN: The Inner Revolution. *Essays on the Social Sciences in History*   TB/1140

EDWARD S. CORWIN: American Constitutional History. *Essays edited by Alpheus T. Mason and Gerald Garvey* △   TB/1136

CARL N. DEGLER, Ed.: Pivotal Interpretations of American History   TB/1240, TB/1241

A. HUNTER DUPREE: Science in the Federal Government: *A History of Policies and Activities to 1940*   TB/573

A. S. EISENSTADT, Ed.: The Craft of American History: *Recent Essays in American Historical Writing*
Vol. I TB/1255; Vol. II TB/1256

CHARLOTTE P. GILMAN: Women and Economics: *A Study of the Economic Relation between Men and Women as a Factor in Social Evolution.* ‡ *Ed. with an Introduction by Carl N. Degler*   TB/3073

OSCAR HANDLIN, Ed.: This Was America: *As Recorded by European Travelers in the Eighteenth, Nineteenth and Twentieth Centuries. Illus.*   TB/1119

MARCUS LEE HANSEN: The Atlantic Migration: 1607–1860. *Edited by Arthur M. Schlesinger*   TB/1052

MARCUS LEE HANSEN: The Immigrant in American History.   TB/1120

JOHN HIGHAM, Ed.: The Reconstruction of American History △   TB/1068

ROBERT H. JACKSON: The Supreme Court in the American System of Government   TB/1106

JOHN F. KENNEDY: A Nation of Immigrants. △ *Illus.*   TB/1118

LEONARD W. LEVY, Ed.: American Constitutional Law: *Historical Essays*   TB/1285

RALPH BARTON PERRY: Puritanism and Democracy   TB/1138

ARNOLD ROSE: The Negro in America   TB/3048

MAURICE R. STEIN: The Eclipse of Community. *An Interpretation of American Studies*   TB/1128

W. LLOYD WARNER and Associates: Democracy in Jonesville: *A Study in Quality and Inequality* ¶   TB/1129

W. LLOYD WARNER: Social Class in America: *The Evaluation of Status*   TB/1013

American Studies: Colonial

BERNARD BAILYN, Ed.: Apologia of Robert Keayne: *Self-Portrait of a Puritan Merchant*   TB/1201

BERNARD BAILYN: The New England Merchants in the Seventeenth Century   TB/1149

JOSEPH CHARLES: The Origins of the American Party System   TB/1049

LAWRENCE HENRY GIPSON: The Coming of the Revolution: 1763–1775. † *Illus.*   TB/3007

LEONARD W. LEVY: Freedom of Speech and Press in Early American History: *Legacy of Suppression*   TB/1109

PERRY MILLER: Errand Into the Wilderness   TB/1139

PERRY MILLER & T. H. JOHNSON, Eds.: The Puritans: *A Sourcebook of Their Writings*
Vol. I TB/1093; Vol. II TB/1094

EDMUND S. MORGAN, Ed.: The Diary of Michael Wigglesworth, 1653–1657: *The Conscience of a Puritan*   TB/1228

EDMUND S. MORGAN: The Puritan Family: *Religion and Domestic Relations in Seventeenth-Century New England*   TB/1227

RICHARD B. MORRIS: Government and Labor in Early America   TB/1244

KENNETH B. MURDOCK: Literature and Theology in Colonial New England   TB/99

WALLACE NOTESTEIN: The English People on the Eve of Colonization: 1603–1630. † *Illus.*   TB/3006

LOUIS B. WRIGHT: The Cultural Life of the American Colonies: 1607–1763. † *Illus.*   TB/3005

American Studies: From the Revolution to 1860

JOHN R. ALDEN: The American Revolution: 1775–1783. † *Illus.*   TB/3011

MAX BELOFF, Ed.: The Debate on the American Revolution, 1761–1783: *A Sourcebook* △   TB/1225

RAY A. BILLINGTON: The Far Western Frontier: 1830–1860. † *Illus.*   TB/3012

W. R. BROCK: An American Crisis: *Congress and Reconstruction, 1865–67* ° △   TB/1283

EDMUND BURKE: On the American Revolution: *Selected Speeches and Letters.* ‡ *Edited by Elliott Robert Barkan*   TB/3068

WHITNEY R. CROSS: The Burned-Over District: *The Social and Intellectual History of Enthusiastic Religion in Western New York, 1800–1850* △   TB/1242

GEORGE DANGERFIELD: The Awakening of American Nationalism: 1815–1828. † *Illus.*   TB/3061

CLEMENT EATON: The Freedom-of-Thought Struggle in the Old South. *Revised and Enlarged. Illus.* TB/1150

CLEMENT EATON: The Growth of Southern Civilization: 1790–1860. † *Illus.*   TB/3040

LOUIS FILLER: The Crusade Against Slavery: 1830–1860. † *Illus.*   TB/3029

DIXON RYAN FOX: The Decline of Aristocracy in the Politics of New York: 1801–1840. ‡ *Edited by Robert V. Remini*   TB/3064

FELIX GILBERT: The Beginnings of American Foreign Policy: *To the Farewell Address*   TB/1200

FRANCIS GRIERSON: The Valley of Shadows: *The Coming of the Civil War in Lincoln's Midwest: A Contemporary Account*   TB/1246

---

† The New American Nation Series, edited by Henry Steele Commager and Richard B. Morris.

‡ American Persectives series, edited by Bernard Wishy and William E. Leuchtenburg.

* The Rise of Modern Europe series, edited by William L. Langer.

¶ Researches in the Social, Cultural, and Behavioral Sciences, edited by Benjamin Nelson.

§ The Library of Religion and Culture, edited by Benjamin Nelson.

Σ Harper Modern Science Series, edited by James R. Newman.

° Not for sale in Canada.

△ Not for sale in the U. K.

FRANCIS J. GRUND: Aristocracy in America: *Social Class in the Formative Years of the New Nation*   TB/1001

ALEXANDER HAMILTON: The Reports of Alexander Hamilton. ‡ *Edited by Jacob E. Cooke*   TB/3060

THOMAS JEFFERSON: Notes on the State of Virginia. ‡ *Edited by Thomas P. Abernethy*   TB/3052

JAMES MADISON: The Forging of American Federalism: *Selected Writings of James Madison. Edited by Saul K. Padover*   TB/1226

BERNARD MAYO: Myths and Men: *Patrick Henry, George Washington, Thomas Jefferson*   TB/1108

JOHN C. MILLER: Alexander Hamilton and the Growth of the New Nation   TB/3057

RICHARD B. MORRIS, Ed.: The Era of the American Revolution   TB/1180

R. B. NYE: The Cultural Life of the New Nation: 1776-1801. † *Illus.*   TB/3026

FRANCIS S. PHILBRICK: The Rise of the West, 1754-1830. † *Illus.*   TB/3067

TIMOTHY L. SMITH: Revivalism and Social Reform: *American Protestantism on the Eve of the Civil War*   TB/1229

FRANK THISTLETHWAITE: America and the Atlantic Community: *Anglo-American Aspects, 1790-1850*   TB/1107

ALBION W. TOURGÉE: A Fool's Errand. ‡ *Ed. by George Fredrickson*   TB/3074

A. F. TYLER: Freedom's Ferment: *Phases of American Social History from the Revolution to the Outbreak of the Civil War. 31 illus.*   TB/1074

GLYNDON G. VAN DEUSEN: The Jacksonian Era: 1828-1848. † *Illus.*   TB/3028

LOUIS B. WRIGHT: Culture on the Moving Frontier   TB/1053

American Studies: The Civil War to 1900

THOMAS C. COCHRAN & WILLIAM MILLER: The Age of Enterprise: *A Social History of Industrial America*   TB/1054

W. A. DUNNING: Essays on the Civil War and Reconstruction. *Introduction by David Donald*   TB/1181

W. A. DUNNING: Reconstruction, Political and Economic: 1865-1877   TB/1073

HAROLD U. FAULKNER: Politics, Reform and Expansion: 1890-1900. † *Illus.*   TB/3020

HELEN HUNT JACKSON: A Century of Dishonor: *The Early Crusade for Indian Reform. ‡ Edited by Andrew F. Rolle*   TB/3063

ALBERT D. KIRWAN: Revolt of the Rednecks: *Mississippi Politics, 1876-1925*   TB/1199

ROBERT GREEN MC CLOSKEY: American Conservatism in the Age of Enterprise: 1865-1910   TB/1137

ARTHUR MANN: Yankee Reformers in the Urban Age: *Social Reform in Boston, 1880-1900*   TB/1247

WHITELAW REID: After the War: *A Tour of the Southern States, 1865-1866. ‡ Edited by C. Vann Woodward*   TB/3066

CHARLES H. SHINN: Mining Camps: *A Study in American Frontier Government. ‡ Edited by Rodman W. Paul*   TB/3062

VERNON LANE WHARTON: The Negro in Mississippi: 1865-1890   TB/1178

American Studies: 1900 to the Present

RAY STANNARD BAKER: Following the Color Line: *American Negro Citizenship in Progressive Era. ‡ Illus. Edited by Dewey W. Grantham, Jr.*   TB/3053

RANDOLPH S. BOURNE: War and the Intellectuals: *Collected Essays, 1915-1919. ‡ Edited by Carl Resek*   TB/3043

A. RUSSELL BUCHANAN: The United States and World War II. † *Illus.*   Vol. I TB/3044; Vol. II TB/3045

ABRAHAM CAHAN: The Rise of David Levinsky: *a documentary novel of social mobility in early twentieth century America. Intro. by John Higham*   TB/1028

THOMAS C. COCHRAN: The American Business System: *A Historical Perspective, 1900-1955*   TB/1080

FOSTER RHEA DULLES: America's Rise to World Power: 1898-1954. † *Illus.*   TB/3021

JOHN D. HICKS: Republican Ascendancy: 1921-1933. † *Illus.*   TB/3041

SIDNEY HOOK: Reason, Social Myths, and Democracy   TB/1237

ROBERT HUNTER: Poverty: *Social Conscience in the Progressive Era. ‡ Edited by Peter d'A. Jones*   TB/3065

WILLIAM L. LANGER & S. EVERETT GLEASON: The Challenge to Isolation: *The World Crisis of 1937-1940 and American Foreign Policy*   Vol. I TB/3054; Vol. II TB/3055

WILLIAM E. LEUCHTENBURG: Franklin D. Roosevelt and the New Deal: 1932-1940. † *Illus.*   TB/3025

ARTHUR S. LINK: Woodrow Wilson and the Progressive Era: 1910-1917. † *Illus.*   TB/3023

GEORGE E. MOWRY: The Era of Theodore Roosevelt and the Birth of Modern America: 1900-1912. † *Illus.*   TB/3022

RUSSEL B. NYE: Midwestern Progressive Politics: *A Historical Study of Its Origins and Development, 1870-1958*   TB/1202

WILLIAM PRESTON, JR.: Aliens and Dissenters: *Federal Suppression of Radicals, 1903-1933*   TB/1287

WALTER RAUSCHENBUSCH: Christianity and the Social Crisis. ‡ *Edited by Robert D. Cross*   TB/3059

JACOB RIIS: The Making of an American. ‡ *Edited by Roy Lubove*   TB/3070

PHILIP SELZNICK: TVA and the Grass Roots: *A Study in the Sociology of Formal Organization*   TB/1230

IDA M. TARBELL: The History of the Standard Oil Company: *Briefer Version. ‡ Edited by David M. Chalmers*   TB/3071

GEORGE B. TINDALL, Ed.: A Populist Reader ‡   TB/3069

TWELVE SOUTHERNERS: I'll Take My Stand: *The South and the Agrarian Tradition. Intro. by Louis D. Rubin, Jr., Biographical Essays by Virginia Rock*   TB/1072

WALTER E. WEYL: The New Democracy: *An Essay on Certain Political Tendencies in the United States. ‡ Edited by Charles B. Forcey*   TB/3042

Anthropology

JACQUES BARZUN: Race: *A Study in Superstition. Revised Edition*   TB/1172

JOSEPH B. CASAGRANDE, Ed.: In the Company of Man: *Twenty Portraits of Anthropological Informants. Illus.*   TB/3047

W. E. LE GROS CLARK: The Antecedents of Man: *Intro. to Evolution of the Primates. ○ △ Illus.*   TB/559

CORA DU BOIS: The People of Alor. *New Preface by the author. Illus.*   Vol. I TB/1042; Vol. II TB/1043

RAYMOND FIRTH, Ed.: Man and Culture: *An Evaluation of the Work of Bronislaw Malinowski ¶ ○ △*   TB/1133

DAVID LANDY: Tropical Childhood: *Cultural Transmission and Learning in a Puerto Rican Village ¶*   TB/1235

L. S. B. LEAKEY: Adam's Ancestors: *The Evolution of Man and His Culture. △ Illus.*   TB/1019

ROBERT H. LOWIE: Primitive Society. *Introduction by Fred Eggan*   TB/1056

EDWARD BURNETT TYLOR: The Origins of Culture. *Part I of "Primitive Culture." § Intro. by Paul Radin*   TB/33

EDWARD BURNETT TYLOR: Religion in Primitive Culture. *Part II of "Primitive Culture." § Intro. by Paul Radin*   TB/34

W. LLOYD WARNER: A Black Civilization: *A Study of an Australian Tribe. ¶ Illus.*   TB/3056

Art and Art History

WALTER LOWRIE: Art in the Early Church. *Revised Edition. 452 illus.*   TB/124

EMILE MÂLE: The Gothic Image: *Religious Art in France of the Thirteenth Century. § △ 190 illus.*   TB/44

MILLARD MEISS: Painting in Florence and Siena after the Black Death: *The Arts, Religion and Society in the Mid-Fourteenth Century. 169 illus.* TB/1148

ERICH NEUMANN: The Archetypal World of Henry Moore. △ *107 illus.* TB/2020

DORA & ERWIN PANOFSKY : Pandora's Box: *The Changing Aspects of a Mythical Symbol. Revised Edition. Illus.* TB/2021

ERWIN PANOFSKY: Studies in Iconology: *Humanistic Themes in the Art of the Renaissance.* △ *180 illustrations* TB/1077

ALEXANDRE PIANKOFF: The Shrines of Tut-Ankh-Amon. *Edited by N. Rambova. 117 illus.* TB/2011

JEAN SEZNEC: The Survival of the Pagan Gods: *The Mythological Tradition and Its Place in Renaissance Humanism and Art. 108 illustrations* TB/2004

OTTO VON SIMSON: The Gothic Cathedral: *Origins of Gothic Architecture and the Medieval Concept of Order.* △ *58 illus.* TB/2018

HEINRICH ZIMMER: Myth and Symbols in Indian Art and Civilization. *70 illustrations* TB/2005

Business, Economics & Economic History

REINHARD BENDIX: Work and Authority in Industry: *Ideologies of Management in the Course of Industrialization* TB/3035

GILBERT BURCK & EDITORS OF FORTUNE: The Computer Age: *And Its Potential for Management* TB/1179

THOMAS C. COCHRAN: The American Business System: *A Historical Perspective, 1900-1955* TB/1080

THOMAS C. COCHRAN: The Inner Revolution: *Essays on the Social Sciences in History* △ TB/1140

THOMAS C. COCHRAN & WILLIAM MILLER: The Age of Enterprise: *A Social History of Industrial America* TB/1054

ROBERT DAHL & CHARLES E. LINDBLOM: Politics, Economics, and Welfare: *Planning and Politico-Economic Systems Resolved into Basic Social Processes* TB/3037

PETER F. DRUCKER: The New Society: *The Anatomy of Industrial Order* △ TB/1082

EDITORS OF FORTUNE: America in the Sixties: *The Economy and the Society* TB/1015

ROBERT L. HEILBRONER: The Great Ascent: *The Struggle for Economic Development in Our Time* TB/3030

FRANK H. KNIGHT: The Economic Organization TB/1214

FRANK H. KNIGHT: Risk, Uncertainty and Profit TB/1215

ABBA P. LERNER: Everybody's Business: *Current Assumptions in Economics and Public Policy* TB/3051

ROBERT GREEN MC CLOSKEY: American Conservatism in the Age of Enterprise, 1865-1910 △ TB/1137

PAUL MANTOUX: The Industrial Revolution in the Eighteenth Century: *The Beginnings of the Modern Factory System in England* ○ △ TB/1079

WILLIAM MILLER, Ed.: Men in Business: *Essays on the Historical Role of the Entrepreneur* TB/1081

RICHARD B. MORRIS: Government and Labor in Early America △ TB/1244

HERBERT SIMON: The Shape of Automation: *For Men and Management* TB/1245

PERRIN STRYKER: The Character of the Executive: *Eleven Studies in Managerial Qualities* TB/1041

PIERRE URI: Partnership for Progress: *A Program for Transatlantic Action* TB/3036

Contemporary Culture

JACQUES BARZUN: The House of Intellect △ TB/1051

CLARK KERR: The Uses of the University TB/1264

JOHN U. NEF: Cultural Foundations of Industrial Civilization △ TB/1024

NATHAN M. PUSEY: The Age of the Scholar: *Observations on Education in a Troubled Decade* TB/1157

PAUL VALÉRY: The Outlook for Intelligence △ TB/1016

RAYMOND WILLIAMS: Culture and Society, 1780-1950 ○ △ TB/1252

RAYMOND WILLIAMS: The Long Revolution.○ △ *Revised Edition* TB/1253

Historiography & Philosophy of History

JACOB BURCKHARDT: On History and Historians. △ *Introduction by H. R. Trevor-Roper* TB/1216

WILHELM DILTHEY: Pattern and Meaning in History: *Thoughts on History and Society.* ○ △ *Edited with an Introduction by H. P. Rickman* TB/1075

J. H. HEXTER: Reappraisals in History: *New Views on History & Society in Early Modern Europe* △ TB/1100

H. STUART HUGHES: History as Art and as Science: *Twin Vistas on the Past* TB/1207

RAYMOND KLIBANSKY & H. J. PATON, Eds.: Philosophy and History: *The Ernst Cassirer Festschrift. Illus.* TB/1115

ARNOLDO MOMIGLIANO: Studies in Historiography ○ △ TB/1288

GEORGE H. NADEL, Ed.: Studies in the Philosophy of History: *Selected Essays from History and Theory* TB/1208

JOSE ORTEGA Y GASSET: The Modern Theme. *Introduction by Jose Ferrater Mora* TB/1038

KARL R. POPPER: The Open Society and Its Enemies △ Vol. I: *The Spell of Plato* TB/1101 Vol. II: *The High Tide of Prophecy: Hegel, Marx and the Aftermath* TB/1102

KARL R. POPPER: The Poverty of Historicism ○ △ TB/1126

G. J. RENIER: History: *Its Purpose and Method* △ TB/1209

W. H. WALSH: Philosophy of History: *An Introduction* △ TB/1020

History: General

L. CARRINGTON GOODRICH: A Short History of the Chinese People. △ *Illus.* TB/3015

DAN N. JACOBS & HANS H. BAERWALD: Chinese Communism: *Selected Documents* TB/3031

BERNARD LEWIS: The Arabs in History △ TB/1029

BERNARD LEWIS: The Middle East and the West ○ △ TB/1274

History: Ancient

A. ANDREWES: The Greek Tyrants △ TB/1103

ADOLF ERMAN, Ed. The Ancient Egyptians: *A Sourcebook of Their Writings. New material and Introduction by William Kelly Simpson* TB/1233

MICHAEL GRANT: Ancient History ○ △ TB/1190

SAMUEL NOAH KRAMER: Sumerian Mythology TB/1055

NAPHTALI LEWIS & MEYER REINHOLD, Eds.: Roman Civilization. *Sourcebook I: The Republic* TB/1231

NAPHTALI LEWIS & MEYER REINHOLD, Eds.: Roman Civilization. *Sourcebook II: The Empire* TB/1232

History: Medieval

P. BOISSONNADE: Life and Work in Medieval Europe: *The Evolution of the Medieval Economy, the 5th to the 15th Century.* ○ △ *Preface by Lynn White, Jr.* TB/1141

HELEN CAM: England before Elizabeth △ TB/1026

NORMAN COHN: The Pursuit of the Millennium: *Revolutionary Messianism in Medieval and Reformation Europe* △ TB/1037

G. G. COULTON: Medieval Village, Manor, and Monastery TB/1022

CHRISTOPHER DAWSON, Ed.: Mission to Asia: *Narratives and Letters of the Franciscan Missionaries in Mongolia and China in the 13th and 14 Centuries* △ TB/315

HEINRICH FICHTENAU: The Carolingian Empire: *The Age of Charlemagne* △ TB/1142

F. L. GANSHOF: Feudalism △ TB/1058

DENO GEANAKOPLOS: Byzantine East and Latin West: *Two Worlds of Christendom in the Middle Ages and Renaissance* TB/1265

EDWARD GIBBON: The Triumph of Christendom in the Roman Empire *(Chaps. XV-XX of "Decline and Fall," J. B. Bury edition).* § △ *Illus.* TB/46

w. o. HASSALL, Ed.: Medieval England: *As Viewed by Contemporaries* △   TB/1205
DENYS HAY: Europe: The Emergence of an Idea   TB/1275
DENYS HAY: The Medieval Centuries ○ △   TB/1192
J. M. HUSSEY: The Byzantine World △   TB/1057
ROBERT LATOUCHE: The Birth of Western Economy: *Economic Aspects of the Dark Ages.* ○ △ *Intro. by Philip Grierson*   TB/1290
FERDINAND LOT: The End of the Ancient World and the Beginnings of the Middle Ages. *Introduction by Glanville Downey*   TB/1044
G. MOLLAT: The Popes at Avignon: 1305-1378 △   TB/308
CHARLES PETIT-DUTAILLIS: The Feudal Monarchy in France and England: *From the Tenth to the Thirteenth Century* ○ △   TB/1165
HENRI PIRENNE: Early Democracies in the Low Countries: *Urban Society and Political Conflict in the Middle Ages and the Renaissance. Introduction by John H. Mundy*   TB/1110
STEVEN RUNCIMAN: A History of the Crusades. △
    Volume I: *The First Crusade and the Foundation of the Kingdom of Jerusalem. Illus.*   TB/1143
    Volume II: *The Kingdom of Jerusalem and the Frankish East, 1100-1187. Illus.*   TB/1243
FERDINAND SCHEVILL: Siena: *The History of a Medieval Commune. Intro. by William M. Bowsky*   TB/1164
SULPICIUS SEVERUS et al.: The Western Fathers: *Being the Lives of Martin of Tours, Ambrose, Augustine of Hippo, Honoratus of Arles and Germanus of Auxerre.* △ *Edited and trans. by F. O. Hoare*   TB/309
HENRY OSBORN TAYLOR: The Classical Heritage of the Middle Ages. *Foreword and Biblio. by Kenneth M. Setton*   TB/1117
F. VAN DER MEER: Augustine The Bishop: *Church and Society at the Dawn of the Middle Ages* △   TB/304
J. M. WALLACE-HADRILL: The Barbarian West: *The Early Middle Ages, A.D. 400-1000* △   TB/1061

History: Renaissance & Reformation

JACOB BURCKHARDT: The Civilization of the Renaissance in Italy. △ *Intro. by Benjamin Nelson & Charles Trinkaus. Illus.*   Vol. I TB/40; Vol. II TB/41
JOHN CALVIN & JACOPO SADOLETO: A Reformation Debate. *Edited by John C. Olin*   TB/1239
ERNST CASSIRER: The Individual and the Cosmos in Renaissance Philosophy. △ *Translated with an Introduction by Mario Domandi*   TB/1097
FEDERICO CHABOD: Machiavelli and the Renaissance △   TB/1193
EDWARD P. CHEYNEY: The Dawn of a New Era, 1250-1453. * *Illus.*   TB/3002
G. CONSTANT: The Reformation in England: *The English Schism, Henry VIII, 1509-1547* △   TB/314
R. TREVOR DAVIES: The Golden Century of Spain, 1501-1621 ○ △   TB/1194
G. R. ELTON: Reformation Europe, 1517-1559 ○ △ TB/1270
DESIDERIUS ERASMUS: Christian Humanism and the Reformation: *Selected Writings. Edited and translated by John C. Olin*   TB/1166
WALLACE K. FERGUSON et al.: Facets of the Renaissance   TB/1098
WALLACE K. FERGUSON et al.: The Renaissance: *Six Essays. Illus.*   TB/1084
JOHN NEVILLE FIGGIS: The Divine Right of Kings. *Introduction by G. R. Elton*   TB/1191
JOHN NEVILLE FIGGIS: Political Thought from Gerson to Grotius: 1414-1625: *Seven Studies. Introduction by Garrett Mattingly*   TB/1032
MYRON P. GILMORE: The World of Humanism, 1453-1517. * *Illus.*   TB/3003
FRANCESCO GUICCIARDINI: Maxims and Reflections of a Renaissance Statesman (Ricordi). *Trans. by Mario Domandi. Intro. by Nicolai Rubinstein*   TB/1160
J. H. HEXTER: More's Utopia: *The Biography of an Idea. New Epilogue by the Author*   TB/1195

HAJO HOLBORN: Ulrich von Hutten and the German Reformation   TB/1238
JOHAN HUIZINGA: Erasmus and the Age of Reformation. △ *Illus.*   TB/19
JOEL HURSTFIELD, Ed.: The Reformation Crisis △ TB/1267
ULRICH VON HUTTEN et al.: On the Eve of the Reformation: *"Letters of Obscure Men." Introduction by Hajo Holborn*   TB/1124
PAUL O. KRISTELLER: Renaissance Thought: *The Classic, Scholastic, and Humanist Strains*   TB/1048
PAUL O. KRISTELLER: Renaissance Thought II: *Papers on Humanism and the Arts*   TB/1163
NICCOLÒ MACHIAVELLI: History of Florence and of the Affairs of Italy: *from the earliest times to the death of Lorenzo the Magnificent. Introduction by Felix Gilbert* △   TB/1027
ALFRED VON MARTIN: Sociology of the Renaissance. *Introduction by Wallace K. Ferguson*   TB/1099
GARRETT MATTINGLY et al.: Renaissance Profiles. △ *Edited by J. H. Plumb*   TB/1162
MILLARD MEISS: Painting in Florence and Siena after the Black Death: *The Arts, Religion and Society in the Mid-Fourteenth Century.* △ *169 illus.*   TB/1148
J. E. NEALE: The Age of Catherine de Medici ○ △ TB/1085
ERWIN PANOFSKY: Studies in Iconology: *Humanistic Themes in the Art of the Renaissance.* △ *180 illustrations*   TB/1077
J. H. PARRY: The Establishment of the European Hegemony: 1415-1715: *Trade and Exploration in the Age of the Renaissance* △   TB/1045
J. H. PLUMB: The Italian Renaissance: *A Concise Survey of Its History and Culture* △   TB/1161
A. F. POLLARD: Henry VIII. ○ △ *Introduction by A. G. Dickens*   TB/1249
A. F. POLLARD: Wolsey. ○ △ *Introduction by A. G. Dickens*   TB/1248
CECIL ROTH: The Jews in the Renaissance. *Illus.* TB/834
A. L. ROWSE: The Expansion of Elizabethan England. ○ △ *Illus.*   TB/1220
GORDON RUPP: Luther's Progress to the Diet of Worms ○ △   TB/120
FERDINAND SCHEVILL: The Medici. *Illus.*   TB/1010
FERDINAND SCHEVILL: Medieval and Renaissance Florence. *Illus.*   Volume I: *Medieval Florence* TB/1090
    Volume II: *The Coming of Humanism and the Age of the Medici*   TB/1091
G. M. TREVELYAN: England in the Age of Wycliffe, 1368-1520 ○ △   TB/1112
VESPASIANO: Renaissance Princes, Popes, and Prelates: *The Vespasiano Memoirs: Lives of Illustrious Men of the XVth Century. Intro. by Myron P. Gilmore*   TB/1111

History: Modern European

FREDERICK B. ARTZ: Reaction and Revolution, 1815-1832. * *Illus.*   TB/3034
MAX BELOFF: The Age of Absolutism, 1660-1815 △   TB/1062
ROBERT C. BINKLEY: Realism and Nationalism, 1852-1871. * *Illus.*   TB/3038
ASA BRIGGS: The Making of Modern England, 1784-1867: *The Age of Improvement* ○ △   TB/1203
CRANE BRINTON: A Decade of Revolution, 1789-1799. * *Illus.*   TB/3018
D. W. BROGAN: The Development of Modern France. ○ △
    Volume I: *From the Fall of the Empire to the Dreyfus Affair*   TB/1184
    Volume II: *The Shadow of War, World War I, Between the Two Wars. New Introduction by the Author*   TB/1185
J. BRONOWSKI & BRUCE MAZLISH: The Western Intellectual Tradition: *From Leonardo to Hegel* △   TB/3001
GEOFFREY BRUUN: Europe and the French Imperium, 1799-1814. * *Illus.*   TB/3033
ALAN BULLOCK: Hitler, A Study in Tyranny. ○ △ *Illus.*   TB/1123

E. H. CARR: German-Soviet Relations Between the Two World Wars, 1919-1939   TB/1278

E. H. CARR: International Relations Between the Two World Wars, 1919-1939 ° △   TB/1279

E. H. CARR: The Twenty Years' Crisis, 1919-1939: An Introduction to the Study of International Relations ° △   TB/1122

GORDON A. CRAIG: From Bismarck to Adenauer: Aspects of German Statecraft. Revised Edition   TB/1171

WALTER L. DORN: Competition for Empire, 1740-1763. * Illus.   TB/3032

FRANKLIN L. FORD: Robe and Sword: The Regrouping of the French Aristocracy after Louis XIV   TB/1217

CARL J. FRIEDRICH: The Age of the Baroque, 1610-1660. * Illus.   TB/3004

RENÉ FUELOEP-MILLER: The Mind and Face of Bolshevism: An Examination of Cultural Life in Soviet Russia. New Epilogue by the Author   TB/1188

M. DOROTHY GEORGE: London Life in the Eighteenth Century △   TB/1182

LEO GERSHOY: From Despotism to Revolution, 1763-1789. * Illus.   TB/3017

C. C. GILLISPIE: Genesis and Geology: The Decades before Darwin §   TB/51

ALBERT GOODWIN: The French Revolution △   TB/1064

ALBERT GUÉRARD: France in the Classical Age: The Life and Death of an Ideal △   TB/1183

CARLTON J. H. HAYES: A Generation of Materialism, 1871-1900. * Illus.   TB/3039

J. H. HEXTER: Reappraisals in History: New Views on History and Society in Early Modern Europe △   TB/1100

STANLEY HOFFMANN et al.: In Search of France: The Economy, Society and Political System in the Twentieth Century   TB/1219

A. R. HUMPHREYS: The Augustan World: Society, Thought, & Letters in 18th Century England ° △   TB/1105

DAN N. JACOBS, Ed.: The New Communist Manifesto and Related Documents. Third edition, revised   TB/1078

HANS KOHN: The Mind of Germany: The Education of a Nation △   TB/1204

HANS KOHN, Ed.: The Mind of Modern Russia: Historical and Political Thought of Russia's Great Age   TB/1065

WALTER LAQUEUR & GEORGE L. MOSSE, Eds.: International Fascism, 1920-1945. ° △ Volume I of Journal of Contemporary History   TB/1276

WALTER LAQUEUR & GEORGE L. MOSSE, Eds.: The Left-Wing Intelligentsia between the Two World Wars. ° △ Volume II of Journal of Contemporary History   TB/1286

FRANK E. MANUEL: The Prophets of Paris: Turgot, Condorcet, Saint-Simon, Fourier, and Comte   TB/1218

KINGSLEY MARTIN: French Liberal Thought in the Eighteenth Century: A Study of Political Ideas from Bayle to Condorcet   TB/1114

L. B. NAMIER: Facing East: Essays on Germany, the Balkans, and Russia in the 20th Century △   TB/1280

L. B. NAMIER: Personalities and Powers: Selected Essays △   TB/1186

L. B. NAMIER: Vanished Supremacies: Essays on European History, 1812-1918 °   TB/1088

JOHN U. NEF: Western Civilization Since the Renaissance: Peace, War, Industry, and the Arts   TB/1113

FRANZ NEUMANN: Behemoth: The Structure and Practice of National Socialism, 1933-1944   TB/1289

FREDERICK L. NUSSBAUM: The Triumph of Science and Reason, 1660-1685. * Illus.   TB/3009

DAVID OGG: Europe of the Ancien Régime, 1715-1783 ° △   TB/1271

JOHN PLAMENATZ: German Marxism and Russian Communism. ° △ New Preface by the Author   TB/1189

RAYMOND W. POSTGATE, Ed.: Revolution from 1789 to 1906: Selected Documents   TB/1063

PENFIELD ROBERTS: The Quest for Security, 1715-1740. * Illus.   TB/3016

PRISCILLA ROBERTSON: Revolutions of 1848: A Social History   TB/1025

GEORGE RUDÉ: Revolutionary Europe, 1783-1815 ° △   TB/1272

LOUIS, DUC DE SAINT-SIMON: Versailles, The Court, and Louis XIV. ° △ Introductory Note by Peter Gay   TB/1250

ALBERT SOREL: Europe Under the Old Regime. Translated by Francis H. Herrick   TB/1121

N. N. SUKHANOV: The Russian Revolution, 1917: Eyewitness Account. △ Edited by Joel Carmichael
Vol. I TB/1066; Vol. II TB/1067

A. J. P. TAYLOR: From Napoleon to Lenin: Historical Essays ° △   TB/1268

A. J. P. TAYLOR: The Habsburg Monarchy, 1809-1918: A History of the Austrian Empire and Austria-Hungary ° △   TB/1187

G. M. TREVELYAN: British History in the Nineteenth Century and After: 1782-1919. ° △ Second Edition TB/1251

H. R. TREVOR-ROPER: Historical Essays ° △   TB/1269

ELIZABETH WISKEMANN: Europe of the Dictators, 1919-1945 ° △   TB/1273

JOHN B. WOLF: The Emergence of the Great Powers, 1685-1715. * Illus.   TB/3010

JOHN B. WOLF: France: 1814-1919: The Rise of a Liberal-Democratic Society   TB/3019

Intellectual History & History of Ideas

HERSCHEL BAKER: The Image of Man: A Study of the Idea of Human Dignity in Classical Antiquity, the Middle Ages, and the Renaissance   TB/1047

R. R. BOLGAR: The Classical Heritage and Its Beneficiaries: From the Carolingian Age to the End of the Renaissance △   TB/1125

RANDOLPH S. BOURNE: War and the Intellectuals: Collected Essays, 1915-1919. △ ‡ Edited by Carl Resek   TB/3043

J. BRONOWSKI & BRUCE MAZLISH: The Western Intellectual Tradition: From Leonardo to Hegel △   TB/3001

ERNST CASSIRER: The Individual and the Cosmos in Renaissance Philosophy. △ Translated with an Introduction by Mario Domandi   TB/1097

NORMAN COHN: The Pursuit of the Millennium: Revolutionary Messianism in Medieval and Reformation Europe △   TB/1037

C. C. GILLISPIE: Genesis and Geology: The Decades before Darwin §   TB/51

G. RACHEL LEVY: Religious Conceptions of the Stone Age and Their Influence upon European Thought. △ Illus. Introduction by Henri Frankfort   TB/106

ARTHUR O. LOVEJOY: The Great Chain of Being: A Study of the History of an Idea   TB/1009

FRANK E. MANUEL: The Prophets of Paris: Turgot, Condorcet, Saint-Simon, Fourier, and Comte △   TB/1218

PERRY MILLER & T. H. JOHNSON, Editors: The Puritans: A Sourcebook of Their Writings
Vol. I TB/1093; Vol. II TB/1094

MILTON C. NAHM: Genius and Creativity: An Essay in the History of Ideas   TB/1196

ROBERT PAYNE: Hubris: A Study of Pride. Foreword by Sir Herbert Read   TB/1031

RALPH BARTON PERRY: The Thought and Character of William James: Briefer Version   TB/1156

GEORG SIMMEL et al.: Essays on Sociology, Philosophy, and Aesthetics. ¶ Edited by Kurt H. Wolff   TB/1234

BRUNO SNELL: The Discovery of the Mind: The Greek Origins of European Thought △   TB/1018

PAGET TOYNBEE: Dante Alighieri: His Life and Works. Edited with Intro. by Charles S. Singleton △   TB/1206

ERNEST LEE TUVESON: Millennium and Utopia: A Study in the Background of the Idea of Progress. ¶ New Preface by the Author   TB/1134

PAUL VALÉRY: The Outlook for Intelligence △   TB/2016

PHILIP P. WIENER: Evolution and the Founders of Pragmatism. △ *Foreword by John Dewey*   TB/1212
BASIL WILLEY: Nineteenth Century Studies: *Coleridge to Matthew Arnold* ○ △   TB/1261
BASIL WILLEY: More Nineteenth Century Studies: *A Group of Honest Doubters* ○ △   TB/1262

Literature, Poetry, The Novel & Criticism

JAMES BAIRD: Ishmael: *The Art of Melville in the Contexts of International Primitivism*   TB/1023
JACQUES BARZUN: The House of Intellect △   TB/1051
W. J. BATE: From Classic to Romantic: *Premises of Taste in Eighteenth Century England*   TB/1036
RACHEL BESPALOFF: On the Iliad   TB/2006
R. P. BLACKMUR et al.: Lectures in Criticism. *Introduction by Huntington Cairns*   TB/2003
JAMES BOSWELL: The Life of Dr. Johnson & The Journal of a Tour to the Hebrides with Samuel Johnson LL.D.: *Selections.* ○ △ *Edited by F. V. Morley. Illus. by Ernest Shepard*   TB/1254
ABRAHAM CAHAN: The Rise of David Levinsky: *a documentary novel of social mobility in early twentieth century America. Intro. by John Higham*   TB/1028
ERNST R. CURTIUS: European Literature and the Latin Middle Ages △   TB/2015
GEORGE ELIOT: Daniel Deronda: *a novel. Introduction by F. R. Leavis*   TB/1039
ADOLF ERMAN, Ed.: The Ancient Egyptians: *A Sourcebook of Their Writings. New Material and Introduction by William Kelly Simpson*   TB/1233
ÉTIENNE GILSON: Dante and Philosophy   TB/1089
ALFRED HARBAGE: As They Liked It: *A Study of Shakespeare's Moral Artistry*   TB/1035
STANLEY R. HOPPER, Ed: Spiritual Problems in Contemporary Literature §   TB/21
A. R. HUMPHREYS: The Augustan World: *Society, Thought and Letters in 18th Century England* ○ △   TB/1105
ALDOUS HUXLEY: Antic Hay & The Giaconda Smile. ○ △ *Introduction by Martin Green*   TB/3503
ALDOUS HUXLEY: Brave New World & Brave New World Revisited. ○ △ *Introduction by Martin Green*   TB/3501
HENRY JAMES: The Tragic Muse: *a novel. Introduction by Leon Edel*   TB/1017
ARNOLD KETTLE: An Introduction to the English Novel. △
Volume I: *Defoe to George Eliot*   TB/1011
Volume II: *Henry James to the Present*   TB/1012
RICHMOND LATTIMORE: The Poetry of Greek Tragedy △   TB/1257
J. B. LEISHMAN: The Monarch of Wit: *An Analytical and Comparative Study of the Poetry of John Donne* ○ △   TB/1258
J. B. LEISHMAN: Themes and Variations in Shakespeare's Sonnets ○ △   TB/1259
ROGER SHERMAN LOOMIS: The Development of Arthurian Romance △   TB/1167
JOHN STUART MILL: On Bentham and Coleridge. △ *Introduction by F. R. Leavis*   TB/1070
KENNETH B. MURDOCK: Literature and Theology in Colonial New England   TB/99
SAMUEL PEPYS: The Diary of Samuel Pepys. ○ *Edited by O. F. Morshead. Illus. by Ernest Shepard*   TB/1007
ST.-JOHN PERSE: Seamarks   TB/2002
V. DE S. PINTO: Crisis in English Poetry, 1880-1940 ○   TB/1260
GEORGE SANTAYANA: Interpretations of Poetry and Religion §   TB/9
C. K. STEAD: The New Poetic: Yeats to Eliot △   TB/1263
HEINRICH STRAUMANN: American Literature in the Twentieth Century. △ *Third Edition, Revised* TB/1168
PAGET TOYNBEE: Dante Alighieri: *His Life and Works. Edited with Intro. by Charles S. Singleton* △ TB/1206
DOROTHY VAN GHENT: The English Novel: *Form and Function*   TB/1050
E. B. WHITE: One Man's Meat. *Introduction by Walter Blair*   TB/3505

BASIL WILLEY: Nineteenth Century Studies: *Coleridge to Matthew Arnold* △   TB/1261
BASIL WILLEY: More Nineteenth Century Studies: *A Group of Honest Doubters* ○ △   TB/1262
RAYMOND WILLIAMS: Culture and Society, 1780-1950 ○ △   TB/1252
RAYMOND WILLIAMS: The Long Revolution. ○ △ *Revised Edition*   TB/1253
MORTON DAUWEN ZABEL, Editor: Literary Opinion in America   Vol. I TB/3013; Vol. II TB/3014

Myth, Symbol & Folklore

JOSEPH CAMPBELL, Editor: Pagan and Christian Mysteries *Illus.*   TB/2013
MIRCEA ELIADE: Cosmos and History: *The Myth of the Eternal Return* § △   TB/2050
MIRCEA ELIADE: Rites and Symbols of Initiation: *The Mysteries of Birth and Rebirth* § △   TB/1236
THEODOR H. GASTER: Thespis: *Ritual, Myth and Drama in the Ancient Near East* △   TB/1281
C. G. JUNG & C. KERÉNYI: Essays on a Science of Mythology: *The Myths of the Divine Child and the Divine Maiden*   TB/2014
DORA & ERWIN PANOFSKY : Pandora's Box: *The Changing Aspects of a Mythical Symbol.* △ *Revised edition. Illus.*   TB/2021
ERWIN PANOFSKY: Studies in Iconology: *Humanistic Themes in the Art of the Renaissance.* △ *180 illustrations*   TB/1077
JEAN SEZNEC: The Survival of the Pagan Gods: *The Mythological Tradition and its Place in Renaissance Humanism and Art.* △ *108 illustrations*   TB/2004
HELLMUT WILHELM: Change: *Eight Lectures on the I Ching* △   TB/2019
HEINRICH ZIMMER: Myths and Symbols in Indian Art and Civilization. △ *70 illustrations*   TB/2005

Philosophy

G. E. M. ANSCOMBE: An Introduction to Wittgenstein's Tractatus. ○ △ *Second Edition, Revised*   TB/1210
HENRI BERGSON: Time and Free Will: *An Essay on the Immediate Data of Consciousness* ○ △   TB/1021
H. J. BLACKHAM: Six Existentialist Thinkers: *Kierkegaard, Nietzsche, Jaspers, Marcel, Heidegger, Sartre* ○ △   TB/1002
CRANE BRINTON: Nietzsche. *New Preface, Bibliography and Epilogue by the Author*   TB/1197
MARTIN BUBER: The Knowledge of Man. △ *Ed. with an Intro. by Maurice Friedman. Trans. by Maurice Friedman and Ronald Gregor Smith*   TB/135
ERNST CASSIRER: The Individual and the Cosmos in Renaissance Philosophy. △ *Translated with an Introduction by Mario Domandi*   TB/1097
ERNST CASSIRER: Rousseau, Kant and Goethe. *Introduction by Peter Gay*   TB/1092
FREDERICK COPLESTON: Medieval Philosophy ○ △   TB/376
F. M. CORNFORD: Principium Sapientiae: *A Study of the Origins of Greek Philosophical Thought. Edited by W. K. C. Guthrie*   TB/1213
F. M. CORNFORD: From Religion to Philosophy: *A Study in the Origins of Western Speculation* §   TB/20
WILFRID DESAN: The Tragic Finale: *An Essay on the Philosophy of Jean-Paul Sartre*   TB/1030
A. P. D'ENTRÈVES: Natural Law: *An Historical Survey* △   TB/1223
MARVIN FARBER: The Aims of Phenomenology: *The Motives, Methods, and Impact of Husserl's Thought*   TB/1291
HERBERT FINGARETTE: The Self in Transformation: *Psychoanalysis, Philosophy and the Life of the Spirit* ¶   TB/1177
PAUL FRIEDLÄNDER: Plato: *An Introduction* △   TB/2017
ÉTIENNE GILSON: Dante and Philosophy   TB/1089
WILLIAM CHASE GREENE: Moira: *Fate, Good, and Evil in Greek Thought*   TB/1104

W. K. C. GUTHRIE: The Greek Philosophers: *From Thales to Aristotle* ° △ TB/1008

F. H. HEINEMANN: Existentialism and the Modern Predicament △ TB/28

ISAAC HUSIK: A History of Medieval Jewish Philosophy JP/3

EDMUND HUSSERL: Phenomenology and the Crisis of Philosophy. *Translated with an Introduction by Quentin Lauer* TB/1170

IMMANUEL KANT: The Doctrine of Virtue, *being Part II of the Metaphysic of Morals. Trans. with Notes & Intro. by Mary J. Gregor. Foreword by H. J. Paton* TB/110

IMMANUEL KANT: Groundwork of the Metaphysic of Morals. *Trans. & analyzed by H. J. Paton* TB/1159

IMMANUEL KANT: Lectures on Ethics. § △ *Introduction by Lewis W. Beck* TB/105

IMMANUEL KANT: Religion Within the Limits of Reason Alone. § *Intro. by T. M. Greene & J. Silber* TB/67

QUENTIN LAUER: Phenomenology: *Its Genesis and Prospect* TB/1169

GABRIEL MARCEL: Being and Having: *An Existential Diary.* △ *Intro. by James Collins* TB/310

GEORGE A. MORGAN: What Nietzsche Means TB/1198

PHILO, SAADYA GAON, & JEHUDA HALEVI: Three Jewish Philosophers. *Ed. by Hans Lewy, Alexander Altmann, &Isaak Heinemann* TB/813

MICHAEL POLANYI: Personal Knowledge: *Towards a Post-Critical Philosophy* △ TB/1158

WILLARD VAN ORMAN QUINE: Elementary Logic: *Revised Edition* TB/577

WILLARD VAN ORMAN QUINE: From a Logical Point of View: *Logico-Philosophical Essays* TB/566

BERTRAND RUSSELL et al.: The Philosophy of Bertrand Russell. *Edited by Paul Arthur Schilpp*
Vol. I TB/1095; Vol. II TB/1096

L. S. STEBBING: A Modern Introduction to Logic △ TB/538

ALFRED NORTH WHITEHEAD: Process and Reality: *An Essay in Cosmology* △ TB/1033

PHILIP P. WIENER: Evolution and the Founders of Pragmatism. *Foreword by John Dewey* TB/1212

WILHELM WINDELBAND: A History of Philosophy
Vol. I: *Greek, Roman, Medieval* TB/38
Vol. II: *Renaissance, Enlightenment, Modern* TB/39

LUDWIG WITTGENSTEIN: The Blue and Brown Books ° TB/1211

Political Science & Government

JEREMY BENTHAM: The Handbook of Political Fallacies: *Introduction by Crane Brinton* TB/1069

KENNETH E. BOULDING: Conflict and Defense: *A General Theory* TB/3024

CRANE BRINTON: English Political Thought in the Nineteenth Century TB/1071

EDWARD S. CORWIN: American Constitutional History: *Essays edited by Alpheus T. Mason and Gerald Garvey* TB/1136

ROBERT DAHL & CHARLES E. LINDBLOM: Politics, Economics, and Welfare: *Planning and Politico-Economic Systems Resolved into Basic Social Processes* TB/3037

JOHN NEVILLE FIGGIS: The Divine Right of Kings. *Introduction by G. R. Elton* TB/1191

JOHN NEVILLE FIGGIS: Political Thought from Gerson to Grotius: *1414-1625: Seven Studies. Introduction by Garrett Mattingly* TB/1032

F. L. GANSHOF: Feudalism △ TB/1058

G. P. GOOCH: English Democratic Ideas in the Seventeenth Century TB/1006

J. H. HEXTER: More's Utopia: *The Biography of an Idea. New Epilogue by the Author* TB/1195

SIDNEY HOOK: Reason, Social Myths and Democracy △ TB/1237

ROBERT H. JACKSON: The Supreme Court in the American System of Government △ TB/1106

DAN N. JACOBS, Ed.: The New Communist Manifesto *and Related Documents. Third Edition, Revised* TB/1078

DAN N. JACOBS & HANS BAERWALD, Eds.: Chinese Communism: *Selected Documents* TB/3031

HANS KOHN: Political Ideologies of the 20th Century TB/1277

ROBERT GREEN MC CLOSKEY: American Conservatism in the Age of Enterprise, 1865-1910 TB/1137

KINGSLEY MARTIN: French Liberal Thought in the Eighteenth Century: *Political Ideas from Bayle to Condorcet* △ TB/1114

ROBERTO MICHELS: First Lectures in Political Sociology. *Edited by Alfred de Grazia* ¶ ° TB/1224

JOHN STUART MILL: On Bentham and Coleridge. △ *Introduction by F. R. Leavis* TB/1070

BARRINGTON MOORE, JR.: Political Power and Social Theory: *Seven Studies* ¶ TB/1221

BARRINGTON MOORE, JR.: Soviet Politics—The Dilemma of Power: *The Role of Ideas in Social Change* ¶ TB/1222

BARRINGTON MOORE, JR.: Terror and Progress—USSR: *Some Sources of Change and Stability in the Soviet Dictatorship* ¶ TB/1266

JOHN B. MORRALL: Political Thought in Medieval Times △ TB/1076

JOHN PLAMENATZ: German Marxism and Russian Communism. ° △ *New Preface by the Author* TB/1189

KARL R. POPPER: The Open Society and Its Enemies △
Vol. I: *The Spell of Plato* TB/1101
Vol. II: *The High Tide of Prophecy: Hegel, Marx and the Aftermath* TB/1102

HENRI DE SAINT-SIMON: Social Organization, The Science of Man, and Other Writings. *Edited and Translated by Felix Markham* TB/1152

JOSEPH A. SCHUMPETER: Capitalism, Socialism and Democracy △ TB/3008

CHARLES H. SHINN: Mining Camps: *A Study in American Frontier Government.* ‡ *Edited by Rodman W. Paul* TB/3062

PETER WOLL, Ed.: Public Administration and Policy: *Selected Essays* TB/1284

Psychology

ALFRED ADLER: The Individual Psychology of Alfred Adler. △ *Edited by Heinz L. and Rowena R. Ansbacher* TB/1154

ALFRED ADLER: Problems of Neurosis. *Introduction by Heinz L. Ansbacher* TB/1145

ANTON T. BOISEN: The Exploration of the Inner World: *A Study of Mental Disorder and Religious Experience* TB/87

ARTHUR BURTON & ROBERT E. HARRIS, Eds.: Clinical Studies of Personality
Vol. I TB/3075; Vol. II TB/3076

HADLEY CANTRIL: The Invasion from Mars: *A Study in the Psychology of Panic* ¶ TB/1282

HERBERT FINGARETTE: The Self in Transformation: *Psychoanalysis, Philosophy and the Life of the Spirit* ¶ TB/1177

SIGMUND FREUD: On Creativity and the Unconscious: *Papers on the Psychology of Art, Literature, Love, Religion.* § △ *Intro. by Benjamin Nelson* TB/45

C. JUDSON HERRICK: The Evolution of Human Nature TB/545

WILLIAM JAMES: Psychology: *The Briefer Course. Edited with an Intro. by Gordon Allport* TB/1034

C. G. JUNG: Psychological Reflections △ TB/2001

C. G. JUNG: Symbols of Transformation: *An Analysis of the Prelude to a Case of Schizophrenia.* △ *Illus.*
Vol. I TB/2009; Vol. II TB/2010

C. G. JUNG & C. KERÉNYI: Essays on a Science of Mythology: *The Myths of the Divine Child and the Divine Maiden* TB/2014

JOHN T. MC NEILL: A History of the Cure of Souls TB/126

KARL MENNINGER: Theory of Psychoanalytic Technique TB/1144

ERICH NEUMANN: Amor and Psyche: *The Psychic Development of the Feminine* △ TB/2012
ERICH NEUMANN: The Archetypal World of Henry Moore. △ *107 illus.* TB/2020
ERICH NEUMANN : The Origins and History of Consciousness △ Vol. I *Illus.* TB/2007; Vol. II TB/2008
C. P. OBERNDORF: A History of Psychoanalysis in America TB/1147
RALPH BARTON PERRY: The Thought and Character of William James: *Briefer Version* TB/1156
JEAN PIAGET, BÄRBEL INHELDER, & ALINA SZEMINSKA: The Child's Conception of Geometry ° △ TB/1146
JOHN H. SCHAAR: Escape from Authority: *The Perspectives of Erich Fromm* TB/1155
MUZAFER SHERIF: The Psychology of Social Norms TB/3072

Sociology

JACQUES BARZUN: Race: *A Study in Superstition. Revised Edition* TB/1172
BERNARD BERELSON, Ed.: The Behavioral Sciences Today TB/1127
ABRAHAM CAHAN: The Rise of David Levinsky: *A documentary novel of social mobility in early twentieth century America. Intro. by John Higham* TB/1028
THOMAS C. COCHRAN: The Inner Revolution: *Essays on the Social Sciences in History* TB/1140
ALLISON DAVIS & JOHN DOLLARD: Children of Bondage: *The Personality Development of Negro Youth in the Urban South* ¶ TB/3049
ST. CLAIR DRAKE & HORACE R. CAYTON: Black Metropolis: *A Study of Negro Life in a Northern City.* △ *Revised and Enlarged. Intro. by Everett C. Hughes*
Vol. I TB/1086; Vol. II TB/1087
EMILE DURKHEIM et al.: Essays on Sociology and Philosophy: *With Analyses of Durkheim's Life and Work.* ¶ *Edited by Kurt H. Wolff* TB/1151
LEON FESTINGER, HENRY W. RIECKEN & STANLEY SCHACHTER: When Prophecy Fails: *A Social and Psychological Account of a Modern Group that Predicted the Destruction of the World* ¶ TB/1132
ALVIN W. GOULDNER: Wildcat Strike: *A Study in Worker-Management Relationships* ¶ TB/1176
FRANCIS J. GRUND: Aristocracy in America: *Social Class in the Formative Years of the New Nation* △ TB/1001
KURT LEWIN: Field Theory in Social Science: *Selected Theoretical Papers.* ¶ △ *Edited with a Foreword by Dorwin Cartwright* TB/1135
R. M. MAC IVER: Social Causation TB/1153
ROBERT K. MERTON, LEONARD BROOM, LEONARD S. COTTRELL, JR., Editors: Sociology Today: *Problems and Prospects* ¶ Vol. I TB/1173; Vol. II TB/1174
ROBERTO MICHELS: First Lectures in Political Sociology. *Edited by Alfred de Grazia* ¶ ° TB/1224
BARRINGTON MOORE, JR.: Political Power and Social Theory: *Seven Studies* ¶ TB/1221
BARRINGTON MOORE, JR.: Soviet Politics—The Dilemma of Power: *The Role of Ideas in Social Change* ¶ TB/1222
TALCOTT PARSONS & EDWARD A. SHILS, Editors: Toward a General Theory of Action: *Theoretical Foundations for the Social Sciences* TB/1083
JOHN H. ROHRER & MUNRO S. EDMONDSON, Eds.: The Eighth Generation Grows Up: *Cultures and Personalities of New Orleans Negroes* ¶ TB/3050
ARNOLD ROSE: The Negro in America: *The Condensed Version of Gunnar Myrdal's An American Dilemma* TB/3048
KURT SAMUELSSON: Religion and Economic Action: *A Critique of Max Weber's The Protestant Ethic and the Spirit of Capitalism.* ¶ ° *Trans. by E. G. French. Ed. with Intro. by D. C. Coleman* TB/1131
PHILIP SELZNICK: TVA and the Grass Roots: *A Study in the Sociology of Formal Organization* TB/1230
GEORG SIMMEL et al.: Essays on Sociology, Philosophy, and Aesthetics. ¶ *Edited by Kurt H. Wolff* TB/1234

HERBERT SIMON: The Shape of Automation: *For Men and Management* △ TB/1245
PITIRIM A. SOROKIN: Contemporary Sociological Theories. *Through the First Quarter of the 20th Century* TB/3046
MAURICE R. STEIN: The Eclipse of Community: *An Interpretation of American Studies* TB/1128
FERDINAND TÖNNIES: Community and Society: *Gemeinschaft und Gesellschaft. Translated and edited by Charles P. Loomis* TB/1116
W. LLOYD WARNER & Associates: Democracy in Jonesville: *A Study in Quality and Inequality* TB/1129
W. LLOYD WARNER: Social Class in America: *The Evaluation of Status* TB/1013

RELIGION

Ancient & Classical

J. H. BREASTED: Development of Religion and Thought in Ancient Egypt. *Intro. by John A. Wilson* TB/57
HENRI FRANKFORT: Ancient Egyptian Religion: *An Interpretation* TB/77
G. RACHEL LEVY: Religious Conceptions of the Stone Age and their Influence upon European Thought. △ *Illus. Introduction by Henri Frankfort* TB/106
MARTIN P. NILSSON: Greek Folk Religion. *Foreword by Arthur Darby Nock* TB/78
ALEXANDRE PIANKOFF: The Shrines of Tut-Ankh-Amon. △ *Edited by N. Rambova. 117 illus.* TB/2011
ERWIN ROHDE: Psyche: *The Cult of Souls and Belief in Immortality Among the Greeks.* △ *Intro. by W. K. C. Guthrie* Vol. I TB/140; Vol. II TB/141
H. J. ROSE: Religion in Greece and Rome △ TB/55

Biblical Thought & Literature

W. F. ALBRIGHT: The Biblical Period from Abraham to Ezra TB/102
C. K. BARRETT, Ed.: The New Testament Background: *Selected Documents* △ TB/86
C. H. DODD: The Authority of the Bible △ TB/43
M. S. ENSLIN: Christian Beginnings △ TB/5
M. S. ENSLIN: The Literature of the Christian Movement △ TB/6
JOHN GRAY: Archaeology and the Old Testament World. △ *Illus.* TB/127
JAMES MUILENBURG: The Way of Israel: *Biblical Faith and Ethics* △ TB/133
H. H. ROWLEY: The Growth of the Old Testament △ TB/107
GEORGE ADAM SMITH: The Historical Geography of the Holy Land. ° △ *Revised and reset* TB/138
D. WINTON THOMAS, Ed.: Documents from Old Testament Times △ TB/85

The Judaic Tradition

LEO BAECK: Judaism and Christianity. *Trans. with Intro. by Walter Kaufmann* JP/23
SALO W. BARON: Modern Nationalism and Religion JP/18
MARTIN BUBER: Eclipse of God: *Studies in the Relation Between Religion and Philosophy* △ TB/12
MARTIN BUBER: For the Sake of Heaven TB/801
MARTIN BUBER: Hasidism and Modern Man. △ *Ed. and Trans. by Maurice Friedman* TB/839
MARTIN BUBER: The Knowledge of Man. △ *Edited with an Introduction by Maurice Friedman. Translated by Maurice Friedman and Ronald Gregor Smith* TB/135
MARTIN BUBER: Moses: *The Revelation and the Covenant* △ TB/837
MARTIN BUBER: The Origin and Meaning of Hasidism △ TB/835
MARTIN BUBER: Pointing the Way. △ *Introduction by Maurice S. Friedman* TB/103
MARTIN BUBER: The Prophetic Faith TB/73
MARTIN BUBER: Two Types of Faith: *the interpenetration of Judaism and Christianity* ° △ TB/75

ERNST LUDWIG EHRLICH: A Concise History of Israel: From the Earliest Times to the Destruction of the Temple in A.D. 70 ° △ TB/128
MAURICE S. FRIEDMAN: Martin Buber: The Life of Dialogue △ TB/64
GENESIS: The NJV Translation TB/836
SOLOMON GRAYZEL: A History of the Contemporary Jews TB/816
WILL HERBERG: Judaism and Modern Man TB/810
ARTHUR HERTZBERG: The Zionist Idea TB/817
ABRAHAM J. HESCHEL: God in Search of Man: A Philosophy of Judaism JP/7
ISAAC HUSIK: A History of Medieval Jewish Philosophy JP/3
FLAVIUS JOSEPHUS: The Great Roman-Jewish War, with The Life of Josephus. Introduction by William R. Farmer TB/74
JACOB R. MARCUS: The Jew in the Medieval World TB/814
MAX I. MARGOLIS & ALEXANDER MARX: A History of the Jewish People TB/806
T. J. MEEK: Hebrew Origins TB/69
C. G. MONTEFIORE & H. LOEWE, Eds.: A Rabbinic Anthology. JP/32
JAMES PARKES: The Conflict of the Church and the Synagogue: The Jews and Early Christianity JP/21
PHILO, SAADYA GAON, & JEHUDA HALEVI: Three Jewish Philosophers. Ed. by Hans Lewey, Alexander Altmann, & Isaak Heinemann TB/813
CECIL ROTH: A History of the Marranos TB/812
CECIL ROTH: The Jews in the Renaissance. Illus. TB/834
HERMAN L. STRACK: Introduction to the Talmud and Midrash TB/808
JOSHUA TRACHTENBERG: The Devil and the Jews: The Medieval Conception of the Jew and its Relation to Modern Anti-Semitism JP/22

Christianity: General

ROLAND H. BAINTON: Christendom: A Short History of Christianity and its Impact on Western Civilization. △ Illus. Vol. I TB/131; Vol. II TB/132

Christianity: Origins & Early Development

AUGUSTINE: An Augustine Synthesis. △ Edited by Erich Przywara TB/335
ADOLF DEISSMANN: Paul: A Study in Social and Religious History TB/15
EDWARD GIBBON: The Triumph of Christendom in the Roman Empire (Chaps. XV-XX of "Decline and Fall," J. B. Bury edition). § △ Illus. TB/46
MAURICE GOGUEL: Jesus and the Origins of Christianity. ° △ Introduction by C. Leslie Mitton
Volume I: Prolegomena to the Life of Jesus TB/65
Volume II: The Life of Jesus TB/66
EDGAR J. GOODSPEED: A Life of Jesus TB/1
ROBERT M. GRANT: Gnosticism and Early Christianity. △ Revised Edition TB/136
ADOLF HARNACK: The Mission and Expansion of Christianity in the First Three Centuries. Introduction by Jaroslav Pelikan TB/92
R. K. HARRISON: The Dead Sea Scrolls : An Introduction ° △ TB/84
EDWIN HATCH: The Influence of Greek Ideas on Christianity. § △ Introduction and Bibliography by Frederick C. Grant TB/18
ARTHUR DARBY NOCK: Early Gentile Christianity and Its Hellenistic Background TB/111
ARTHUR DARBY NOCK: St. Paul ° △ TB/104
ORIGEN: On First Principles. △ Edited by G. W. Butterworth. Introduction by Henri de Lubac TB/311
JAMES PARKES: The Conflict of the Church and the Synagogue: The Jews and Early Christianity JP/21
SULPICIUS SEVERUS et al.: The Western Fathers: Being the Lives of Martin of Tours, Ambrose, Augustine of Hippo, Honoratus of Arles and Germanus of Auxerre. △ Edited and translated by F. R. Hoare TB/309

F. VAN DER MEER: Augustine the Bishop: Church and Society at the Dawn of the Middle Ages △ TB/304
JOHANNES WEISS: Earliest Christianity: A History of the Period A.D. 30-150. Introduction and Bibliography by Frederick C. Grant Volume I TB/53
Volume II TB/54

Christianity: The Middle Ages and The Reformation

JOHN CALVIN & JACOPO SADOLETO: A Reformation Debate. Edited by John C. Olin TB/1239
G. CONSTANT: The Reformation in England: The English Schism, Henry VIII, 1509-1547 △ TB/314
CHRISTOPHER DAWSON, Ed.: Mission to Asia: Narratives and Letters of the Franciscan Missionaries in Mongolia and China in the 13th and 14th Centuries △ TB/315
JOHANNES ECKHART: Meister Eckhart: A Modern Translation by R. B. Blakney TB/8
DESIDERIUS ERASMUS: Christian Humanism and the Reformation: Selected Writings. Edited and translated by John C. Olin TB/1166
ÉTIENNE GILSON: Dante and Philosophy △ TB/1089
WILLIAM HALLER: The Rise of Puritanism △ TB/22
HAJO HOLBORN: Ulrich von Hutten and the German Reformation TB/1238
JOHAN HUIZINGA: Erasmus and the Age of Reformation. △ Illus. TB/19
A. C. MCGIFFERT: Protestant Thought Before Kant △ Preface by Jaroslav Pelikan TB/93
JOHN T. MCNEILL: Makers of the Christian Tradition: From Alfred the Great to Schleiermacher △ TB/121
G. MOLLAT: The Popes at Avignon, 1305-1378 △ TB/308
GORDON RUPP: Luther's Progress to the Diet of Worms ° △ TB/120

Christianity: The Protestant Tradition

KARL BARTH: Church Dogmatics: A Selection △ TB/95
KARL BARTH: Dogmatics in Outline △ TB/56
KARL BARTH: The Word of God and the Word of Man TB/13
RUDOLF BULTMANN et al: Translating Theology into the Modern Age: Historical, Systematic and Pastoral Reflections on Theology and the Church in the Contemporary Situation. Volume 2 of Journal for Theology and the Church, edited by Robert W. Funk in association with Gerhard Ebeling TB/252
WHITNEY R. CROSS: The Burned-Over District: The Social and Intellectual History of Enthusiastic Religion in Western New York, 1800-1850 △ TB/1242
WINTHROP HUDSON: The Great Tradition of the American Churches TB/98
SOREN KIERKEGAARD: On Authority and Revelation: The Book on Adler. Translated by Walter Lowrie. Intro. by Frederick Sontag TB/139
SOREN KIERKEGAARD: Edifying Discourses. Edited with an Introduction by Paul Holmer TB/32
SOREN KIERKEGAARD: The Journals of Kierkegaard. ° △ Ed. with Intro. by Alexander Dru TB/52
SOREN KIERKEGAARD: The Point of View for My Work as an Author: A Report to History. § Preface by Benjamin Nelson TB/88
SOREN KIERKEGAARD: The Present Age. § △ Translated and edited by Alexander Dru. Introduction by Walter Kaufmann TB/94
SOREN KIERKEGAARD: Purity of Heart △ TB/4
SOREN KIERKEGAARD: Repetition: An Essay in Experimental Psychology. △ Translated with Introduction & Notes by Walter Lowrie TB/117
SOREN KIERKEGAARD: Works of Love: Some Christian Reflections in the Form of Discourses § TB/122
WALTER LOWRIE: Kierkegaard: A Life Vol. I TB/89
Vol. II TB/90
JOHN MACQUARRIE: The Scope of Demythologizing: Bultmann and his Critics △ TB/134

PERRY MILLER & T. H. JOHNSON, Editors: The Puritans: *A Sourcebook of Their Writings*   Vol. I   TB/1093
   Vol. II   TB/1094
JAMES M. ROBINSON et al.: The Bultmann School of Biblical Interpretation: New Directions? *Volume 1 of Journal for Theology and the Church, edited by Robert W. Funk in association with Gerhard Ebeling*
   TB/251
F. SCHLEIERMACHER: The Christian Faith. △ *Introduction by Richard R. Niebuhr*   Vol. I   TB/108
   Vol. II   TB/109
F. SCHLEIERMACHER: On Religion: *Speeches to Its Cultured Despisers. Intro. by Rudolf Otto*   TB/36
TIMOTHY L. SMITH: Revivalism and Social Reform: *American Protestantism on the Eve of the Civil War*
   TB/1229
PAUL TILLICH: Dynamics of Faith △   TB/42
PAUL TILLICH: Morality and Beyond   TB/142
EVELYN UNDERHILL: Worship △   TB/10
G. VAN DER LEEUW: Religion in Essence and Manifestation: *A Study in Phenomenology.* △ *Appendices by Hans H. Penner*   Vol. I   TB/100; Vol. II   TB/101

Christianity: The Roman and Eastern

Traditions

DOM CUTHBERT BUTLER: Western Mysticism: *The Teaching of Augustine, Gregory and Bernard on Contemplation and the Contemplative Life* § ○ △   TB/312
A. ROBERT CAPONIGRI, Ed.: Modern Catholic Thinkers I: *God and Man* △   TB/306
A. ROBERT CAPONIGRI. Ed.: Modern Catholic Thinkers II: *The Church and the Political Order*△   TB/307
THOMAS CORBISHLEY, S.J.: Roman Catholicism △   TB/112
CHRISTOPHER DAWSON: The Historic Reality of Christian Culture   TB/305
G. P. FEDOTOV: The Russian Religious Mind: *Kievan Christianity, the 10th to the 13th centuries*   TB/370
G. P. FEDOTOV, Ed.: A Treasury of Russian Spirituality
   TB/303
ÉTIENNE GILSON: The Spirit of Thomism   TB/313
DAVID KNOWLES: The English Mystical Tradition △
   TB/302
GABRIEL MARCEL: Being and Having: *An Existential Diary.* △ *Introduction by James Collins*   TB/310
GABRIEL MARCEL: Homo Viator: *Introduction to a Metaphysic of Hope*   TB/397
FRANCIS DE SALES: Introduction to the Devout Life. *Trans. by John K. Ryan*   TB/316
GUSTAVE WEIGEL, S. J.: Catholic Theology in Dialogue
   TB/301

Oriental Religions: Far Eastern, Near Eastern

TOR ANDRAE: Mohammed: *The Man and His Faith* △
   TB/62
EDWARD CONZE: Buddhism: *Its Essence and Development.* ○ △ *Foreword by Arthur Waley*   TB/58
EDWARD CONZE et al., Editors: Buddhist Texts Through the Ages △   TB/113
ANANDA COOMARASWAMY: Buddha and the Gospel of Buddhism. △ *Illus.*   TB/119
H. G. CREEL: Confucius and the Chinese Way   TB/63
FRANKLIN EDGERTON, Trans. & Ed.: The Bhagavad Gita
   TB/115
SWAMI NIKHILANANDA, Trans. & Ed.: The Upanishads: *A One-Volume Abridgment* △   TB/114
HELLMUT WILHELM: Change: *Eight Lectures on the I Ching* △   TB/2019

Philosophy of Religion

NICOLAS BERDYAEV: The Beginning and the End § △ TB/14
NICOLAS BERDYAEV: Christian Existentialism: *A Berdyaev Synthesis.* △ *Ed. by Donald A. Lowrie*   TB/130
NICOLAS BERDYAEV: The Destiny of Man △   TB/61
RUDOLF BULTMANN: History and Eschatology: *The Presence of Eternity* ○   TB/91

RUDOLF BULTMANN AND FIVE CRITICS: Kerygma and Myth: *A Theological Debate* △   TB/80
RUDOLF BULTMANN and KARL KUNDSIN: Form Criticism: *Two Essays on New Testament Research.* △ *Translated by Frederick C. Grant*   TB/96
MIRCEA ELIADE: The Sacred and the Profane   TB/81
LUDWIG FEUERBACH: The Essence of Christianity. § *Introduction by Karl Barth. Foreword by H. Richard Niebuhr*   TB/11
ÉTIENNE GILSON: The Spirit of Thomism   TB/313
ADOLF HARNACK: What is Christianity? § △ *Introduction by Rudolf Bultmann*   TB/17
FRIEDRICH HEGEL: On Christianity: *Early Theological Writings. Ed. by R. Kroner and T. M. Knox*   TB/79
KARL HEIM: Christian Faith and Natural Science △ TB/16
IMMANUEL KANT: Religion Within the Limits of Reason Alone. § *Intro. by T. M. Greene & J. Silber*   TB/67
K. E. KIRK: The Vision of God: *The Christian Doctrine of the Summum Bonum* § △   TB/137
JOHN MACQUARRIE: An Existentialist Theology: *A Comparison of Heidegger and Bultmann.* ○ △ *Preface by Rudolf Bultmann*   TB/125
PAUL RAMSEY, Ed.: Faith and Ethics: *The Theology of H. Richard Niebuhr*   TB/129
PIERRE TEILHARD DE CHARDIN: The Divine Milieu ○ △
   TB/384
PIERRE TEILHARD DE CHARDIN: The Phenomenon of Man ○ △   TB/383

Religion, Culture & Society

JOSEPH L. BLAU, Ed.: Cornerstones of Religious Freedom in America: *Selected Basic Documents, Court Decisions and Public Statements. Revised and Enlarged Edition*   TB/118
C. C. GILLISPIE: Genesis and Geology: *The Decades before Darwin* §   TB/51
KYLE HASELDEN: The Racial Problem in Christian Perspective   TB/116
WALTER KAUFMANN, Ed.: Religion from Tolstoy to Camus: *Basic Writings on Religious Truth and Morals. Enlarged Edition*   TB/123
JOHN T. MC NEILL: A History of the Cure of Souls TB/126
KENNETH B. MURDOCK: Literature and Theology in Colonial New England   TB/99
H. RICHARD NIEBUHR: Christ and Culture △   TB/3
H. RICHARD NIEBUHR: The Kingdom of God in America
   TB/49
R. B. PERRY: Puritanism and Democracy   TB/1138
PAUL PFUETZE: Self, Society, Existence: *Human Nature and Dialogue in the Thought of George Herbert Mead and Martin Buber*   TB/1059
WALTER RAUSCHENBUSCH: Christianity and the Social Crisis. ‡ *Edited by Robert D. Cross*   TB/3059
KURT SAMUELSSON: Religion and Economic Action: *A Critique of Max Weber's* The Protestant Ethic and the Spirit of Capitalism ¶ ○ △ *Trans. by E. G. French. Ed. with Intro. by D. C. Coleman*   TB/1131
TIMOTHY L. SMITH: Revivalism and Social Reform: *American Protestantism on the Eve of the Civil War* △
   TB/1229
ERNST TROELTSCH: The Social Teaching of the Christian Churches ○ △   Vol. I   TB/71; Vol. II   TB/72

NATURAL SCIENCES
AND MATHEMATICS

Biological Sciences

CHARLOTTE AUERBACH: The Science of Genetics Σ △
   TB/568
MARSTON BATES: The Natural History of Mosquitoes. *Illus.*   TB/578
A. BELLAIRS: Reptiles: *Life History, Evolution, and Structure.* △ *Illus.*   TB/520
LUDWIG VON BERTALANFFY: Modern Theories of Development: *An Introduction to Theoretical Biology* TB/554

LUDWIG VON BERTALANFFY: Problems of Life: *An Evaluation of Modern Biological and Scientific Thought* △
TB/521
HAROLD F. BLUM: Time's Arrow and Evolution   TB/555
JOHN TYLER BONNER: The Ideas of Biology. Σ △ *Illus.*
TB/570
A. J. CAIN: Animal Species and their Evolution. △ *Illus.*
TB/519
WALTER B. CANNON: Bodily Changes in Pain, Hunger, Fear and Rage. *Illus.*   TB/562
W. E. LE GROS CLARK: The Antecedents of Man: *An Introduction to Evolution of the Primates.* o △ *Illus.* TB/559
W. H. DOWDESWELL: Animal Ecology. △ *Illus.*   TB/543
W. H. DOWDESWELL: The Mechanism of Evolution. △ *Illus.*
TB/527
R. W. GERARD: Unresting Cells. *Illus.*   TB/541
DAVID LACK: Darwin's Finches. △ *Illus.*   TB/544
ADOLF PORTMANN: Animals as Social Beings. o △ *Illus.*
TB/572
O. W. RICHARDS: The Social Insects. △ *Illus.*   TB/542
P. M. SHEPPARD: Natural Selection and Heredity. △ *Illus.*
TB/528
EDMUND W. SINNOTT: Cell and Psyche: *The Biology of Purpose*   TB/546
C. H. WADDINGTON: How Animals Develop. △ *Illus.*
TB/553
C. H. WADDINGTON: The Nature of Life: *The Main Problems and Trends in Modern Biology* △   TB/580

Chemistry

J. R. PARTINGTON: A Short History of Chemistry. △ *Illus.*
TB/522

Communication Theory

J. R. PIERCE: Symbols, Signals and Noise: *The Nature and Process of Communication* △   TB/574

Geography

R. E. COKER: This Great and Wide Sea: *An Introduction to Oceanography and Marine Biology. Illus.*   TB/551
F. K. HARE: The Restless Atmosphere △   TB/560

History of Science

MARIE BOAS: The Scientific Renaissance, 1450-1630 o △
TB/583
W. DAMPIER, Ed.: Readings in the Literature of Science. *Illus.*   TB/512
A. HUNTER DUPREE: Science in the Federal Government: *A History of Policies and Activities to 1940* △ TB/573
ALEXANDRE KOYRÉ: From the Closed World to the Infinite Universe: *Copernicus, Kepler, Galileo, Newton, etc.* △
TB/31
A. G. VAN MELSEN: From Atomos to Atom: *A History of the Concept* Atom   TB/517
O. NEUGEBAUER: The Exact Sciences in Antiquity △ TB/552
HANS THIRRING: Energy for Man: *From Windmills to Nuclear Power* △   TB/556
STEPHEN TOULMIN & JUNE GOODFIELD: The Architecture of Matter: *Physics, Chemistry & Physiology of Matter, Both Animate & Inanimate, As it Evolved Since the Beginning of Science* o △   TB/584
STEPHEN TOULMIN & JUNE GOODFIELD: The Discovery of Time o △   TB/585
LANCELOT LAW WHYTE: Essay on Atomism: *From Democritus to 1960* △   TB/565

Mathematics

E. W. BETH: The Foundations of Mathematics: *A Study in the Philosophy of Science* △   TB/581
H. DAVENPORT: The Higher Arithmetic: *An Introduction to the Theory of Numbers* △   TB/526
H. G. FORDER: Geometry: *An Introduction* △   TB/548
S. KÖRNER: The Philosophy of Mathematics: *An Introduction* △   TB/54/
D. E. LITTLEWOOD: Skeleton Key of Mathematics: *A Simple Account of Complex Algebraic Problems* △
TB/525
GEORGE E. OWEN: Fundamentals of Scientific Mathematics   TB/569
WILLARD VAN ORMAN QUINE: Mathematical Logic TB/558
O. G. SUTTON: Mathematics in Action. o △ *Foreword by James R. Newman. Illus.*   TB/518
FREDERICK WAISMANN: Introduction to Mathematical Thinking. *Foreword by Karl Menger*   TB/511

Philosophy of Science

R. B. BRAITHWAITE: Scientific Explanation   TB/515
J. BRONOWSKI: Science and Human Values. △ *Revised and Enlarged Edition*   TB/505
ALBERT EINSTEIN et al.: Albert Einstein: Philosopher-Scientist. *Edited by Paul A. Schilpp* Vol. I TB/502
Vol. II TB/503
WERNER HEISENBERG: Physics and Philosophy: *The Revolution in Modern Science* △   TB/549
JOHN MAYNARD KEYNES: A Treatise on Probability. o △ *Introduction by N. R. Hanson*   TB/557
KARL R. POPPER: Logic of Scientific Discovery △   TB/576
STEPHEN TOULMIN: Foresight and Understanding: *An Enquiry into the Aims of Science.* △ *Foreword by Jacques Barzun*   TB/564
STEPHEN TOULMIN: The Philosophy of Science: *An Introduction* △   TB/513
G. J. WHITROW: The Natural Philosophy of Time o o △
TB/563

Physics and Cosmology

JOHN E. ALLEN: Aerodynamics: *A Space Age Survey* △
TB/582
STEPHEN TOULMIN & JUNE GOODFIELD: The Fabric of the Heavens: *The Development of Astronomy and Dynamics.* △ *Illus.*   TB/579
DAVID BOHM: Causality and Chance in Modern Physics. △ *Foreword by Louis de Broglie*   TB/536
P. W. BRIDGMAN: Nature of Thermodynamics   TB/537
P. W. BRIDGMAN: A Sophisticate's Primer of Relativity △
TB/575
A. C. CROMBIE, Ed.: Turning Point in Physics   TB/535
C. V. DURELL: Readable Relativity. △ *Foreword by Freeman J. Dyson*   TB/530
ARTHUR EDDINGTON: Space, Time and Gravitation: *An Outline of the General Relativity Theory*   TB/510
GEORGE GAMOW: Biography of Physics Σ △   TB/567
MAX JAMMER: Concepts of Force: *A Study in the Foundation of Dynamics*   TB/550
MAX JAMMER: Concepts of Mass *in Classical and Modern Physics*   TB/571
MAX JAMMER: Concepts of Space : *The History of Theories of Space in Physics. Foreword by Albert Einstein*   TB/533
G. J. WHITROW: The Structure and Evolution of the Universe: *An Introduction to Cosmology.* △ *Illus.* TB/504